BILLY BARTRAM

and His Green World

BILLY BARTRAM

AND HIS GREEN WORLD

An Interpretative Biography by

MARJORY BARTLETT

SANGER

Farrar, Straus & Giroux

NEW YORK

The illustrations in this volume are reproduced from *William
Bartram: Botanical and Zoological Drawings, 1756–1788,* introduction
and notes by Joseph Ewan (Memoirs Amer. Philos. Soc. 74, 1968), plates
14, 17, 20, 21, 22, 23, 27, 29, 30, 32, 37, 40, 42, 45, and 49,
by kind permission of the American Philosophical Society and of the Trustees
of the British Museum (Natural History). The original drawings are in
the British Museum.

Foreword

⚮

Two hundred years ago our land was torn asunder by the controversy of whether or not to undertake the step of separation from our mother country. Then, the decision for separation made, the new patriots became engaged in a perilous war for their independence.

Far from that particular turmoil, a young man rode off into the unexplored wilderness and into another kind of turmoil. But Billy Bartram rode with joy and took a true delight in all he met. And he returned with an awe and a wonder which he recorded for all time.

Who was William Bartram? To say that he was an artist, a writer, a naturalist, a traveler is not enough. To say that he was the son of the Royal Botanist, who was a companion of Benjamin Franklin, is not enough either. Nor does the fact that he himself was host to Washington and Jefferson adequately describe him.

Still, the question of who William Bartram was is asked sufficiently often to warrant a comprehensive answer. Most of all, the man deserves a degree of the appreciation he spent so freely upon others.

No biography can ever portray a person exactly. An interpretative biography not only reports the known events of a man's life but also tries, whenever possible, to explore and even to explain them. In this sense, it assumes some of the aspects of the historical novel.

It is vital, therefore, that the author assure her readers that she has in no instance willfully misled them by distorting facts or introducing scenes or dialogues that are out of character with the people involved.

Casual conversations are seldom, if ever, recorded, but written material is often saved. Many of the remarks that my characters make have come from their letters or other documents. In the case of Franklin and Jefferson, written materials were not difficult to find. Much of the correspondence between John Bartram and his English patron, Peter Collinson, has been preserved, as have some of William Bartram's letters. The advice that John gives to Billy upon his departure for North Carolina actually derives from a letter which Billy wrote years later to his nephew, but it is not unlikely that he could have heard these same words from his father.

By far the most valuable clue to Billy's character and personality, he himself has left us in his *Travels*. It was mainly from his own writings that I drew his portrait.

An interpretative study by its very nature needs to be selective; therefore, omissions are inevitable. At the same time, it is always a temptation to choose incidents and to draw conclusions that might cast fresh light.

But the author has a more important commitment, and that is to state truthfully, compassionately, and succinctly what must be said. This is what I have endeavored to do. That through all the facts and figures Billy Bartram's endearing spirit constantly shines is a circumstance over which I had no control.

Marjory Bartlett Sanger

Winter Park, Florida
June 1971

Acknowledgments

Two people have done more to make this book possible than I know how to acknowledge adequately. Emily Read Cheston of Ambler, Pennsylvania, a member of the John Bartram Association's board, sent me rare and out-of-print books from the association's library, together with photographs, letters, and maps. All of these proved invaluable to me in my work.

In Philadelphia, Mrs. Cheston took me upon several occasions to the Bartram house and garden. She showed me my first Franklinia. It is no exaggeration to say that without her and the John Bartram Association, this biography could not have been written.

My other special assistance came from Wanda Suggs Campbell, historian and clerk at the Bladen County Court House in Elizabethtown, North Carolina. Mrs. Campbell took a week's vacation to drive me over the county—to Ashwood, to the Walnut Grove and Oakland plantations, to Carvers Creek, to Moore's Creek Bridge, and to the grave of Mary, deep in the woods above the Cape Fear River. She gave me old and new books, copies of documents, and photographs, and she introduced me to descendants of the Bartrams and Robesons. I owe her more than I can say.

Across the ocean, Lt. Col. Brian D. Mackenzie spent hours in the British Museum of Natural History, engaged in painstaking research for me. I hope he knows how grateful I am.

Miss Winifred Ballachey, M.B.E., of Kew, Surrey, was most helpful in putting me in touch with Sir George Taylor, Director of the Royal Botanic Gardens there.

Of the more than a hundred books I have read in connection with this work, three have been real guideposts. I should like to express special appreciation to Mrs. Helen Gere Cruickshank for *John and William Bartram's America,* to Dr. Francis Harper for his Naturalist's Edition of the *Travels,* and to Professor Joseph Ewan, editor of *William Bartram: Botanical and Zoological Drawings.*

In addition to all the above, I must also express gratitude for the interest and aid of Dr. John B. Bartram; Mr. Philip R. Bartram; Mr. John Hanby Debnam, President of the Lower Cape Fear Historical Society; Mrs. Henry C. Evans of the John Bartram Association; Mrs. Ida B. Kellam, Archivist of the Lower Cape Fear Historical Society; Mr. John D. Kilbourne of the Historical Society of Pennsylvania; Dr. Hugh T. Lefler; and Mr. Edward R. Manners of the Wilson Ornithological Society, who pointed out to me my first and only *Bartramia longicauda.*

Finally, I feel that I cannot conclude these acknowledgments without mentioning the forebearance of H. D. Vursell, my editor. This book consumed far more time than I had anticipated, and throughout the delays I received only encouragement and understanding.

Contents

Illustrations

❧

BILLY BARTRAM
and His Green World

CHAPTER 1

THE FARMER
OF KINGSESSING

"Slave to no sect, who takes no private road,
But looks through Nature up to Nature's God."

Alexander Pope

The sun that summer afternoon glazed the river with light. Here and there, on the meadow banks, leafy oaks and maples cast a green shade. John Bartram, hoeing a bed of plants that he had carried in his saddlebag all the way from the Catskill Mountains, straightened up and looked out at the river. The year was 1755, and John Bartram was fifty-six years old.

He had traveled widely for his time, and he was planning to travel again. But he was most content when he was working in his garden. Born in the last year of the seventeenth century, he had grown up on a farm not far from where he now lived. Here, at Kingsessing on the Schuylkill, the "Hidden River" of the Dutch, he had built his fieldstone house with his own hands, enlarging a Swedish settler's tiny building already there, quarrying and hewing the stone from his new fields. On an ever-spreading segment of his several hundred acres, he had planned and planted his beloved garden. And all the while he had taught his large family to love nature and particularly God, the Creator, from whom he earnestly believed everything sprang.

Unknown to John, one of his children was at that very moment unexpectedly near at hand. Billy Bartram, during his summer vacation from Mr. Franklin's Old College in Philadelphia, had been trying to earn some money by working on a neighbor's farm. But just the day before, he had started a drawing of a scarlet tanager on its nest, and now he must hurry to finish before the eggs hatched and the bird became busy with feeding. Tanagers had nested in that tulip tree in the garden a year ago, and Billy could not help wondering whether they might not be the same birds.

Safely obscured behind a lilac hedge, he had been in hiding. But when he looked through a frame of branches and saw his father working in the heat of the afternoon and then standing and gazing at the cool river, he had a sudden impulse to go and offer him some sort of thanks for his kindness and patience with him, the most disappointing of his children.

Billy, at sixteen, was old enough to know that he had failed to fulfill his parents' expectations of him. His poor marks, stemming from his inattentiveness at school, had been hard for them to understand. It seemed that, as the out-of-doors became more and more important to him, figures and figuring became more and more meaningless.

Laying his English drawing pad carefully on the grass, and rising cautiously so as not to disturb the bird on its nest, Billy was about to step through the hedge when he saw that he would not be alone on the path. Striding from the house and down through the garden came a familiar portly figure. Billy ducked back into the lilac just in time.

John Bartram had not noticed his son, but he stared with amazement, mixed with some dismay, at his approaching guest. As usual, the visitor was unannounced. And there was little doubt that the farmer of Kingsessing, as Mr. Franklin had referred to him because of the settlement in which he lived, would be roundly scolded for his labors in the hot sun.

"So, John, Mrs. Bartram was correct. She told me I should find thee in thy garden at this hour. I could scarcely believe her. Yet here thee is." Benjamin Franklin was not a Quaker, as the Bartrams were, but with his old friend he used the familiar "plain language."

John leaned his hoe against the bald cypress tree that he had brought years ago from Delaware as a switch stuck in his boot. "Ben, Ben, this is a welcome surprise. But thee should have attended me in the house. Johnny would have fetched me. Fortunately, Ann is understanding about my gardening; thee should not have to suffer for my folly."

Franklin replied dryly that he hoped Mrs. Bartram would be as understanding when she was a widow.

John smiled and took his caller's arm. "We'll seek some shade. And thee must sample the cider from those New York apple trees sent from Dr. Colden's." With little difficulty he urged his guest up the path.

Ben Franklin strode into an arbor where grape leaves mingled with a twining trumpet creeper sent by John's half brother in North Carolina. He sighed as he settled himself on the hand-hewn bench. He was, he professed, deeply troubled by the stirrings of unrest and dissatisfaction evidenced of late by the colonies against the mother country. He was also disturbed by the languishing of his Philosophic Society, "through the idleness of its members, though neither thee nor I," he reported to Bartram.

More than ten years before, Franklin had organized a Society for the Promotion of Useful Knowledge, which later became widely known and honored as the American Philosophical Society. John, representing the science of agriculture, was a charter member and concerned with "all new-discovered plants, herbs, trees, roots, their virtues, uses, etc; methods of propagating them and making them useful."

Comfortable at last in the shaded arbor, the two friends droned on like the bees overhead in the trellis. A sudden breeze from the river stirred the dark leaves, making an undulating pattern on the stone floor; wasps swung in circles over the ripening grapes. Mrs. Ann Bartram brought mugs of cold cider and left the men to themselves.

Although from different backgrounds and different cultures—one a product of the city, the other the country; one sophisticated, the other provincial—the two men had much in common. In the eighteenth century a growing interest in the natural world had involved far-flung scientists in a kind of international fraternity.

A moving spirit in this widespread group was a London wool merchant and amateur botanist named Peter Collinson. Across the Atlantic on nearly every ship went Collinson's packages of seeds and roots, with his letters carefully wrapped in dry tobacco leaves to discourage the nibbling of insects.

In return, packages for his own garden made their arduous trip to London.

John Bartram and Peter Collinson had never met, but through their mutual friend, Ben Franklin, Peter had become interested in John, and then, gradually, had become his benefactor. Over the years Peter had sought to procure for him British patrons, wealthy noblemen who were anxious to add American plants to their landscape parks and perennial borders. Gardening in England had become fashionable and competitive; owners and designers of great estates were constantly on the lookout for something unusual.

John revealed to Mr. Franklin that the latest shipment of seeds from Kingsessing had not been acknowledged by the always punctilious Collinson. "I trust that they were not swept overboard," he worried. "Among them were those Solomon's Seals that he reminded me had escaped me before, and a walking stick he requested made of the Canewood. I also included a packet of butterflies which Peter prefers before beetles, there being ten times the beauty and variety in one as in the other."

Franklin reminded his conscientious companion that Peter Collinson had not yet fully recovered from the shock of the death of his wife at forty-nine. At that time John had sent word to his "dear afflicted friend" that God knew what was best for our ultimate good and that, living in love and innocency, we might die in hope.

More practically, Franklin had written that "the best remedy of grief is time."

Still, John fretted about the packages he had shipped to England. For five guineas a box, he sent whatever plants, roots, and seeds he could find on his wilderness journeys. All were apparently welcome. But rats on the boats would chew at them, and so would "pestilent beetles"; dampness would rot them, storm waves would engulf them. Often they would be left in their wrappings to sprout on the wharves. For every plant that eventually flourished in its new environment, countless others were lost.

Collinson fretted about these losses too, and also about what he considered John's country manners. He cautioned John against disgracing either of them by going unhandsomely garbed into Virginia to call upon Mr. Custis or Mr. Byrd. Virginians were genteel and well-dressed people, Peter had tried to explain, and never mind the expense, he would send him more clothes. And yet, John remembered, looking down the garden slopes, some neat, some weedy, to where the Schuylkill reflected the bright sky, when he had offered to his steward, Harvey, a cap that Peter had sent with a hole in the brim, Collinson had reprimanded him for not having returned it for his own use out-of-doors in rainy weather.

Hearing this, Franklin had remarked that the wealthiest were often the thriftiest, and therein might lie the reason for their wealth.

Collinson was also critical of John Bartram's grammar and spelling, even to the extent of overlooking his botanical specimens to chide him about the manner and expression of his descriptions. John in return protested that correct grammar and spelling pleased only those who preferred a fine superficial flourish to the honest fact.

In truth, Collinson, for all his concern and kindness, was not noted for his tact. Some years before, he had written to Sir Hans Sloane, president of the Royal Society, asking him to donate seashells to him, "for," as he put it, "if it should please the Great Dispenser of our being to remove you, all my hopes of ever obtaining anything of that kind vanishes."

But it must also be acknowledged that, particularly when in the presence of men like Franklin, John was overly sensitive about his lack of formal education. In the little settlement of Marple, near Darby, Pennsylvania, where Bartram was born, there had only been a small country school.

John's grandfather had come from Derbyshire, England, with William Penn in 1682 to farm in the New World, and farming had been the only life John ever knew. His mother had died when he was two; his father then moved to North Carolina, leaving his son to be brought up by his grandmother. Their farm at Marple was all-important to them, and when his grandmother died she left it to John.

At twenty-nine he went to a sheriff's sale and there he bought slightly over one hundred acres. Later he added more. The land was at Kingsessing, close by Gray's Ferry, where a much-traveled road led to the rapidly growing city of Philadelphia, about four miles away. Philadelphia was at that time the unquestioned cultural center of the colonies.

The two friends, lulled by the warmth of the afternoon and the droning of insects, sat in quiet thought.

"One might imagine," John said at last, "that Peter would be pleased at the Library Company's generosity in lending me books, especially since he is its agent. But alas, no. He is now afraid that too much reading on my part will rob me of time for plant collecting. He even wrote to remind me of the advice of Solomon: 'In reading books there is no end.'"

Franklin suggested dryly that John could reply to Collinson, "Had King Solomon loved women less and reading more, he might have been still wiser than he was." He dispatched the cider that had come from John's own press and mill, hand-cut from solid rock at the river's edge, and he prepared to depart. In spite of the pleasing tenor of the day, he was unable to relax for more than an hour or so.

Ever since his kite experiment in electricity three years ago—an experiment which, incidentally, had caused his friend John to scold him severely for the risk he took, although it had gained him membership in the Royal Society —Benjamin Franklin had had many demands upon his time. A true product of his environment and of the eighteenth century, he was a man of many parts, deeply involved in the development of scientific and philosophical concepts, and of course in politics and the future of the colonies.

Just recently Franklin's primary concern had been with the increasing anxiety that the peace-loving Pennsylvania Society of Friends felt about the American Indians taking sides with the French and setting out on the warpath. Exactly one year ago, had he not been engaged in trying to secure adequate supplies for General Braddock, that "good mechanical soldier" who was totally unpracticed in the techniques of waging war in Indian-haunted woods? At the same time Franklin found a moment to send to Peter Collinson a "few cakes of American soap, made of myrtle wax, said to be the best soap in the world for shaving, or washing fine linens." In return, he had requested enough satin for a lady's gown.

Even now, Franklin suspected, he might have to go at any time into Indian territory to confer with the chiefs of the tribes. Bartram himself had been sent several years ago by James Logan, William Penn's secretary and a most influential statesman, to the Council of the Five Nations in the hope of securing peace. Then the Alleghenies, where he rode, had been mapped simply as "The Endless Mountains." Now Logan, who almost fifty years before had introduced Isaac Newton's principles to the New World, was dead, and his library of two thousand priceless volumes was bequeathed to the city of Philadelphia.

John Bartram actually had little sympathy for the Indians. He showed, in fact, an astonishingly un-Quakerlike hostility toward them. The only proper way to treat an Indian, he avowed, was to bang him stoutly and aplenty.

This was an element in his friend's philosophy that Franklin had difficulty understanding. John excused his own attitude by protesting that the savage Indians kept him out of woods where he longed to go plant hunting. The explanation did not entirely satisfy his friends. It seemed to them that something deeper and more disturbing must provoke such uncharacteristic antagonism.

"Oh, Pennsylvania!" John had recently declaimed. "Thou that wert the most flourishing and peaceable province in North America, art now scourged by the most barbarous creatures in the universe."

Ben had pointed out that the Indians were not the sole troublemakers. A year before, it had seemed that the French might be planning to take the capital, then at Philadelphia. John, who sadly maintained that his fellow townspeople cared more for their furniture, silver, and china than for their gardens, had declared that "two twenty-two gun ships could take the town in two hours' time," so "at ease and dissolved in luxury" were its citizens.

Now, on this summer afternoon with the sun beating down on the fields of hay, clover, and flax along the river, Mr. Franklin rose to leave. John reached out a quick hand to restrain him. There was something else on his mind which he must discuss with his mercurial friend. He called to Ann for more cider. This time it was brought by his slender, dark-haired daughter Elizabeth, who had begged for the privilege of serving their distinguished guest. Franklin, thanking her, recognized her as Billy's twin.

John was pleased that Ben should remember each of his many children. He admitted on Elizabeth's departure that it was about Billy he wished to talk. It was no secret that the father was worried. Billy, at sixteen, had shown no interest in choosing a profession or even in continuing his education. Drawing was his "darling delight," his father sighed.

This was not the first time that the two men had pondered the future of John's shy, artistic son. Several years ago Franklin had offered to teach Billy the art of printing and to find him a teacher in engraving. With the boy's skill and ingenuity in drawing and design, he had said, he might well make a satisfactory engraver, and certainly it was a profitable trade. But unless Billy would determine to "settle close," and apply himself, it would never answer the good purpose intended.

John had only smiled and shaken his head at the offer, protesting that Ben was the only printer that did ever make a livelihood by it in this place.

Just the past winter the concerned father had sent, through Peter Collinson, a letter to the learned Dr. Gronovius at the University of Leiden in Holland, saying that he had "a little son about fifteen years of age that has travelled with me now three years; & already he knows most of ye plants that grows in our four governments he hath drawn most of our oaks & birches with a draught of ye drownded lands & several of ye adjacent mountains & rivers as they appeared to him in his journey by them . . . he hath drawn several birds before when he could find a little time from school where he learns Latin."

To this letter Peter Collinson had added a postscript before sending it on. "His sons Drawings are very fine. I wish they could be published."

But nothing was heard from Gronovius.

Now John had a new worry about this strange son of his. It was a deep-seated fear that one day his restlessness would compel him to leave the safe haven of his home and venture forth on dangerous and difficult paths, possibly with no knowledge of where he was going. He mentioned this to his friend, knowing full well that Ben, at Billy's age, had fled his Boston home to escape to Philadelphia.

John remembered the summer two years before, when he had taken Billy "botanizing" with him in the Catskills. Ever since then he believed that he had seen the longing for travel in Billy's eyes. That, combined with his son's love of collecting and of drawing plants and animals, led his anxious father to fear that Billy would not be content to linger indefinitely on the shores of this slow-moving river.

Birds were calling and plummeting like stones into the trees. Butterflies drifted across the fields. It was hard for John Bartram to conceive that one could not be content forever in such a place. Yet, as he had confided to Benjamin Franklin and others, he did not wish that any of his sons be "what is commonly called a gentleman, and have no occupation." Actually, for several years he had dreamed that Billy might become a physician.

Once he himself had yearned to become a doctor. Had he been able to obtain the education that Billy had at Old College, he would have studied physic and surgery. As it was, he had some knowledge of medicinal herbs and their uses and curative powers. That was, he admitted, what had turned him toward botany. From time to time he had even medically treated his neighbors who for one reason or another had been unable to engage physicians from the city.

Peter Collinson had suggested surveying as an occupation in which Billy could find the freedom he longed for, as well as the chance to explore his beloved wilderness. But John had replied sadly that "we have five times more surveyers already than can get half employ."

He squinted off into the soft glare toward the glossy-leaved magnolia trees that he had brought from his journey to the Indian country of the Five Nations. "If Peter could find patrons for Billy's drawings as he found patrons for my plants, I should no longer worry," he told Franklin wistfully.

This reminded Franklin of something else. John Bartram, he often thought, had, with his large family, more worries than those solely about Billy. What John needed, of course, was more patrons, not only abroad but in this country as well. Franklin had advertised for him in his newspaper, but with little result. Some settlers had brought bulbs from their own English borders and seemed content with these and nothing more. Gardening, many thought, was a luxury they could ill afford until they became better established. Others imported the familiar plants of their homeland.

But an idea far more ambitious had formed in Franklin's mind. What if he could arrange for a Royal Appointment for his diligent and deserving friend? What if Bartram might be made Botanist to the King? Was there not a possibility that with the aid of Collinson, and a few others of the brotherhood of patrons and scientists, something might be managed? It was a pity that Sir Hans Sloane was no longer alive.

Physician to George II, as well as president of the Royal Society, Sloane had died two years before at ninety-three. His collection of scientific curios, which Collinson helped to arrange, had already become the nucleus of the British Museum. Bartram had sent many specimens to Sir Hans, always carefully labeled as: "This grass I found growing by A creak in A rich bottom in ye indian countrey near Susquehana"; "this variegated fern I found in ye countrey of ye 5 nations on flat moist ground"; or "this we call ditany & hath been used with good success in curing ye bite of A rattle snake." They were further marked: "Specimens colected by John Bartram in ye year 1742 for Sir Hance Sloan."

At his friend's suggestion of the Royal Appointment, John shrugged modestly, but in truth it was an honor for which he had yearned more than once. "They say the gardens of the Prince and Princess of Wales at Kew need little more than is already planted there," he ventured, by way of some sort of excuse or explanation.

Franklin did not agree. He had visions of the mother country burgeoning with American blooms. John's word "gardens" caused him to inquire if he knew where Billy might be at this moment. John replied that he was haying in a neighbor's field.

Benjamin Franklin rose once more. He had remained, he said, far longer than he had intended, but his friend's good company and hospitality, not to mention the shade of the arbor and the prospect from it, had proved irresistible. The cider was still the finest in the colony. He would return with pleasure when he was able, he went on, but he should not be expected soon. Matters both here and abroad were becoming extremely serious. Much as he regretted having to say so, he sensed the winds of war were in the air.

He added then that, if urgently needed, young Billy might

be found where there was little if any hay, under the tulip tree by the hedge. As usual, his bright eye had missed nothing.

Billy Bartram had completed his drawing of the scarlet tanager on its nest. The bird had cooperated by sitting almost motionless among the broad, blunt-ended leaves, of which Billy had also drawn a few separate samples for Mr. Collinson, along with those of the American sugar maple.

He knew, too, how to draw birds on the wing, particularly the great hawks that soared and sailed down the valley in the fall of the year. Movement entranced him, the movement of drifting leaves, wind-blown branches, grasses bending, and particularly the waterfalls that he had seen in the mountains where his father had taken him.

More than anything else Billy longed to travel into the wilderness again. But now it was apparently too dangerous. Ferocious Indians lurked on every trail. They would kill any white man they met, his father told him.

Billy had trouble believing this. He had seen only a few Indians. His father had seen many and been with them at their councils, where they had been courteous to him; and yet his father was a wise man and must be right in his opinions. Still, it was confusing to Billy, who envied and admired the Indians for their freedom and their knowledge of nature, their ability to find their way, and to survive in wild places.

In the distance he heard the voices of his two younger brothers, John and Benjamin, as they worked in the garden. Young John was the one who cared most of all about farming. Already his father had given him some farmland of his own. Billy remembered this with a sudden flush of shame.

He had overheard his father say, "My John is a worthy, sober, industrious son and delights in plants." Why, wondered Billy, could I have not been that way? He did delight in plants, perhaps even more than John, but he knew all too well that he was neither worthy nor industrious. Had not Mr. Thomson and his other teachers said so many times? Had not his own father indicated it?

Still, Mr. Collinson had confidence in him. Remembering this, and his request for drawings and descriptions, Billy picked up his tablet and made his way along a secluded path to the river. Thus it was that he missed his father, who arrived at the tulip tree a few minutes later.

John could not help being pleased that for once his eminent friend Benjamin Franklin had been mistaken. Billy might not be industrious or gifted in figuring, but he was respectful, obedient, and loving, and it was not to be supposed that he would deceive his father by remaining home from work. If Ben saw anyone at all, it was doubtless either young John or Benjamin, his namesake.

John Bartram went back to hoeing the row where his friend had found him. The sun was lower now; cooler breezes came from the river. Even so, John would not have been deterred. He had completely recovered from the fever which had plagued him during his trip through the Catskills with Billy two years before. It had been his idea to show to this restless, gifted son of his a broken, mountainous landscape quite unlike the rolling meadows of eastern Pennsylvania.

But at that time John, tired from fighting his illness, though reluctant to admit it, had been happy to arrive at Coldenham, the Hudson River estate of his friend Dr. Cadwallader Colden, the Scottish medical doctor who became the first Surveyor General of the colonies and later Lieutenant Governor of New York. Although in his remote retreat he was constantly exposed to marauding Indians, Dr. Colden had been surprisingly at home with them. He had written a revealing report entitled "History of the Five Indian Nations of Canada which are dependent on the province of New York and which are the barrier between the English and French," and he was an acknowledged authority on the Iroquois. Yet after the publication of the history, he had written to Bartram that, for a while at least, his botanical pleasures had been stopped and he dared not venture out alone for fear of having his scalp taken.

John had visited Dr. Colden before, because they had much in common in their interest in botany and in the planting of gardens. John found the doctor's knowledge of medicinal herbs helpful in furthering his own theories about the curative value of native plants. In turn, Dr. Colden praised his new friend's lively fancy, surprising memory, and indefatigable disposition. So he was delighted to welcome him when he arrived with his son in the summer of 1753.

It was a memorable visit. Also arriving was Dr. Alexander Garden of Charleston, another Scottish physician and botanist, whose name was to be immortalized in the fragrant gardenia. They spoke of men whose names were already well known.

Dr. Colden had received a letter from the Swedish botanist and taxonomist Linnaeus, in which he explained that he was taking "the liberty of writing in order to begin a correspondence for which I have long wished, but never found the means of beginning."

And Dr. Garden, on his return to South Carolina, wrote to Linnaeus: "How happy should I be to pass my life with men so distinguished by genius, acuteness and liberality as well as by eminent botanical learning and experience."

Carl von Linné, whose surname his father had chosen from the stately linden tree, was the famous professor of medicine who had planted the botanical garden at the University of Uppsala, where he taught. He had, several years before, published his revolutionary and controversial *Systema Naturae,* the binomial system of plant classification based on the number of pistils and stamens. Each species was assigned to a genus and identified by two descriptive Latin names, Latin being the universal scientific language.

Linné had endeavored to introduce method and order into the uncharted mazes of botany and, some said, rescue the whole field from chaos. "God created, Linné set in order," declared his supporters. Gronovius had his book published in Holland at his own expense and sent a copy to Bartram.

Not everyone was happy to have the mazes charted and the old names changed. Dr. Johann Jakob Dillenius of Oxford called the young Swede "a man who is bringing all botany into confusion." Peter Collinson, always ready with an opinion, had written to Linnaeus asserting that it gave botanists pain to see the familiar words lost forever and that if he would be constantly altering old and good names for new ones that conveyed no idea of the plant, it would be impossible to attain to a perfect knowledge in a science which formerly had been a "pleasant study and attainable, by most men." To his unseen friend John Bartram he had complained that this "coining of a new set of names for plants tends but to embarrass and perplex the study of Botany."

Dr. Colden introduced this topic as the men, with Billy among them, sat conversing after dinner in his elegant drawing room with its polished English furniture and damask curtains. Outside, the wind beat through the pines that Indians had marked for their trails, paths originally created by wolf and fox and deer.

Typically, John Bartram took the side of his benefactor. "You will think," he ventured, "that I uphold him because he has obtained noble patrons for me in England, beginning with the late Lord Petre." He paused. It had been a sad day for both Bartram and Collinson when Petre had died suddenly of smallpox in his thirtieth year. Collinson had been moved to write to John, lamenting that he had loved Petre more like a brother than a friend, that indeed he was dearer to him than all men.

Bartram went on: "Lady Petre appears to have shared her husband's interests. She has sent requests for plants as well as sending to me the seeds of a most excellent and thriving pear tree. In return for her kindness I procured for her pleasure a hummingbird's nest with eggs inside, and a pair of dried birds to place beside it. The son also, the ninth Lord Petre, is very like his father. He wishes wasps' nests with dead wasps within, and living terrapins for his pond at Thorndon, in Essex. In this respect, Peter wrote that 'it may truly be said the spirit of Elijah rests upon Elisha.' "

John realized that he had strayed a bit far afield in this discussion. "Peter's real grievance with Linnaeus appears to be a personal one," he said, trying to pick up the thread of the conversation. "It seems that for many years he has sent to him in Sweden plants and fossils without ever a single specimen in exchange. He only recently complained to me that Dr. Linnaeus receives all and returns little, whereas he, as he readily admits, is like a parson's barn, refusing nothing."

Dr. Garden smiled and included Billy in his glance. "You peaceable Quakers, always smoothing troubled waters, always fair to everybody."

And Billy could not help smiling too, wondering how much fairness the young doctor would find in his father's opinion of the Indians.

"Collinson should have no grievance at all," Dr. Garden went on. "Did not Linnaeus name for him that lemon-scented yellow woodland mint we were content to call horse balm? Now I suppose we must learn to say *Collinsonia,* in honor of dear Peter. Indeed, John, it was you who found the plant and sent it across the ocean. By every right it should have been named *Bartramia.*"

Dr. Colden, to whom Collinson had once written that John Bartram was "a wonderful natural genius," vigorously agreed with Alexander Garden, but John put up his hand. "Come," he protested, "Peter wasted no time in letting me know that he believed I was more deserving of the honor than he was, and that he had already 'writ to Linnaeus not to forget the pains and travels of John Bartram but to stick a feather in his cap, who is as deserving as the rest.' "

"A feather," observed Colden dryly, "is about all he is likely to offer."

John was far less concerned for himself than his friends were. "Peter was delighted with his *Collinsonia,*" he said gently. "He told me that he had thanked Linnaeus for having been so good as to give him a species of eternity, botanically speaking—a name for as long as men and books endure."

"Humph!" retorted Dr. Colden. "In any case, it is but a poor plant, with an insignificant blossom. I never yet saw it soothe a horse or any other animal, and Peter Kalm vows that he cannot pass anywhere near where it is growing without suffering the most violent of headaches."

Billy Bartram could not suppress a laugh. He was feeling unusually elated. It was as though he had sampled some of the Madeira at dinner. But he required no wine. It was exhilarating enough to be sitting with these men and hearing them speak of others who were only legends to him.

It had also been exhilarating that afternoon to talk to Dr. Colden's daughter Jane, who, although older than Billy, had taken the time to spend several hours with him, showing him her botanical drawings and telling him of her walks through the woods on Indian trails, searching for native wild flowers.

She had even asked him to send her some of his own plant pictures, and Billy had resolved then and there to make a whole collection for her. They had sat side by side on the steps of the wide porch and watched the shadow of the deep wood, in which there were thrushes singing, progress toward them across the lawn.

With some difficulty Billy drew himself back to the present. His father, for whom the horse balm had not been named, was as usual being fair and firm about it, protesting that it was a splendid plant, curing a variety of ills, and going on to describe how he had observed Indians boiling it to drink as a remedy for rattlesnake bite. Indians and rattlesnakes never seemed far from his mind.

Billy remembered that a few days before, at the summit of a rocky precipice, he had been about to kick at a remarkably patterned fungus when his watchful father had pulled him back, crying, "Rattlesnake!" Although he had heard of them all his life, this was the first that Billy had ever seen, and he was not too terrified to marvel at the beauty of its speckled, patterned skin. That night, while his father was drying seeds by the campfire and labeling his specimens, Billy had drawn by the flickering light in careful detail that rattlesnake both from memory and from the skin which his father had preserved.

"And what of the Lapland plant Linné named for himself," John was saying, "which he described as 'depressed, hairy, neglected, and flowering only for a brief time'?"

"Yet look what Linnaeus did for Kalm," Colden retorted, still fuming at what he considered an injustice to his friend, Bartram.

Billy knew that plant. It was the beautiful mountain laurel, *Kalmia latifolia,* with its waxy evergreen leaves and starlike pink and white blossoms that opened in the wild places by the dark pines and firs and hemlocks in the ravines where crystal waterfalls plunged into leaf-clogged pools.

And he was glad that the conversation had turned to Peter Kalm. This traveling student of Dr. Linnaeus had been his hero since that day when Kalm had visited his father's farm a few years before. Billy leaned forward and rested his forehead in his thin hand. His eyes burned, and he felt unnaturally warm. Actually he was feeling a little dizzy, although nothing would induce him to admit it. It was the excitement of the evening, he told himself, and being on this long-dreamed-of trip with his father, and listening now, with the Hudson River wind at every window, to a conversation of botanists that he would never forget.

Neither had he forgotten Peter Kalm's arrival at Kingsessing, although Billy had been just a child at the time. There had recently been more famous people who had made pilgrimages to the garden: Mr. Franklin and the members of his scientific society, Dr. Colden, Mr. Logan, and Dr. John Mitchell from Virginia, among others. But there was something special about the blond adventurous young foreigner who had come to Philadelphia for a brief visit and stayed eight months. During which time, James Logan complained to Collinson, Kalm cared to see nobody except Franklin and Bartram.

The Scandinavian naturalist was, on his part, even more enthusiastic about the Bartrams than they were about him. He endeared himself to the large sociable family, admiring John's self-taught Latin, which enabled him to read the scientific books he longed to, and his wide knowledge of botany and practical farming. He was particularly entertained and instructed by his host's understanding of the medicinal powers of his native woodland plants: alder and poke and sassafras. He was surprised, he admitted naïvely, to find in America what he called a "compleat man."

On visiting Collinson in London afterwards and reading his copy of John Bartram's *Journal of the Five Nations and the Lake Ontario*, Kalm had expressed keen disappointment. "Why," he exclaimed, "he has not filled it with a thousandth part of his great knowledge!"

It had been in September when Kalm had come to Kingsessing, and although bitten by insects until he felt himself disfigured, and kept awake at night by choruses of frogs from the river, he professed to have nothing but pleasure in what he saw. Writing to Collinson, who had never crossed the ocean and longed to, Linnaeus's student reported that he had come into a whole new world. "Wherever I looked to the ground," Kalm said, "I everywhere found such plants as I had never seen before."

The peaches in John Bartram's orchard filled him with awe. "Might I please pluck one?" in his newly learned English he asked young Billy, who trailed him everywhere he went. And Billy, to show him how much he admired him and how welcome he was to anything he wished, had scrambled up the tree and filled both hands with the ripest fruit he could find.

"Stop, stop," the visitor had then implored. "In my country, only the very rich can afford to eat them, they are so scarce. Pick no more for me, I beg you. It would not seem right if I were to return to Uppsala feeling wealthy."

"John!" Billy heard a voice drifting through what had appeared to be the autumn haze of the peach orchard. "Look to Billy. He is either asleep or not well."

With some pain Billy roused himself. Besides the dizziness which increased and the sudden ache in his head, he had the familiar sensations of sorrow and shame. He had enjoyed this evening at Coldenham more than any since Peter Kalm had come to Kingsessing so long ago. Now none of these gentlemen would believe him. And, worse than that, he had disgraced his father once more.

Yet it was his father who professed to be ashamed. "I forgot that this is but a boy," he told them. "A lad of fourteen who has come for the first time on a long journey. Forgive me, Billy; and pray do not tell thy mother that I overlooked thy bedtime."

But in the corridor outside his room he laid his hand on Billy's forehead. "My son," he said, "thy cheek is too rosy, and thy eye is overbright. I fear that thy brow is heated. Can it be that thee has caught a trace of my old fever? If so, I have herbs with me . . ."

"Father, I am deeply sorry that I disgraced thee before those gentlemen. What will they think of thee now?"

And then his father had put his hand on his head again, but in a different way, not seeking whether there was a fever to be cured with his herbs. "They will think, Billy Bartram, that I am a fortunate man indeed to have such a son as my companion."

By morning's light there was no doubt that Billy had a fever. Dr. Colden urged fervently that the boy and his father stay on with him. He could provide poultices and tisanes from the plants in his garden; he was, after all, a physician, as was his other guest, Dr. Garden. There was everything in the house to make the patient comfortable indefinitely. "Under what more propitious circumstances could one be ill?" he demanded.

His daughter Jane was equally insistent; Billy must stay. She knew something of nursing, and then as he recuperated she would teach him from her knowledge of drawing, and they would undertake easy jaunts into the fields and woods to search for new plants for him to sketch.

John Bartram, though, prevailed. His strong face with its firm chin and steady eyes reflected determination as well as anxiety. "Billy needs to be at home," he said. "We shall post there with all haste."

Now, two summers later, Billy was still prone to illnesses. It worried him that he was not as strong as the other boys in his classes. On the farm where he was supposed to be working as a laborer, he could complete little more than half of the tasks that were set out for him. He did not mention this at home. He knew that, in spite of his mother's concern, his father expected and desired him to be strong. And certainly he would have to be if he were ever to travel with his father again.

And how he did delight in travel. It seemed to him then, as he peered down into the tea-colored water of the Schuyl-kill, looking for turtles and water snakes, that he had never been happier than in those days when he had ridden with his father into the mountains of New York. Even his sudden fever had not dulled his joy in it.

He thought often of Dr. Colden's daughter, Jane. Although only fourteen, he had been experienced enough to recognize her botanical drawings as simple and wanting in polish, yet she had cared enough to venture into dangerous Indian territory to look for plants and sketch them. She was the first woman artist that he had ever met, and he admired her very much. True to his resolve, he had made a packet of drawings for her, which his father, on viewing them, had called "very fine."

Now, thinking of Jane and remembering the waterfalls, dark pools, and rocky crevices of those northern woods where thrushes sang at dusk, he was filled with an unfamiliar sense of discontent. He loved his father's house and was proud of his famous garden, but all at once it seemed like a prison to him. For the first time he understood his older brother Moses's having left home to seek adventure and new scenes. All had not gone well for Moses, though, and eventually he had been forced to seek help from Mr. Collinson in London. That patient gentleman bought him a suit of clothes and paid his passage back to Philadelphia, but at least Moses had traveled.

Billy gazed bleakly up and down the riverbank. Ordinarily the landscape would have enthralled him. Gauzy-winged dragonflies hovered over blue beds of pickerelweed; sunfish glittered through the reeds. Here and there a stalk of cardinal flower stood like a red sentinel.

From a low branch of a willow hanging over the water, a phoebe was fly-catching. Chestnut-sided and golden-winged warblers piped brief snatches of their spring songs, and catbirds and yellowthroats skulked in the alders.

A couple of mud turtles were sunning on a half-submerged log, and a huge old snapper lazed through the brown shallows, but Billy had drawn them many times; they were nothing new. He looked back at the gray phoebe, flicking its tail, waiting, then when the opportunity came, darting off to snatch its prey, and returning, always returning, to the same perch over the river.

Near the cypress tree in the garden Billy found his father. "Had thee come earlier, thee would have seen Mr. Franklin," said John. "As usual, although he professed that all he desired was to sit in the shade and refresh himself with a mug of cider, he was soon pressed and impatient to be on his way. Nevertheless, he had much of interest to impart, including a whirlwind he had seen."

Storms had always held a fascination for Billy; his father knew this. "What whirlwind, and where?" he wanted to know.

"Why, one that he recently encountered while riding through Maryland with Colonel Tasker and his party. Not the least put off by it, as the others were sensible enough to be, and purporting to wish to 'examine' the phenomenon, he followed it closely enough to strike at it with his whip, until he marked that it was breaking off large limbs and even tree trunks and scattering them nearby. On inquiring of his host if such whirlwinds were commonplace in Maryland, he was charmed to be informed that this one had been purposefully ordered in his honor."

Billy could not help laughing; this was so typical of Mr. Franklin.

"He further informed me that he intended to burden Mr. Collinson with a detailed report of his experience, using the excuse that the long-suffering Peter was as intrigued with wind gusts as he was. 'Burden' and 'long-suffering' are my words, not Mr. Franklin's," John added.

Billy still laughed, but at the mention of Mr. Collinson his soft eyes took on a faraway look.

"Wind gusts were not all that we discussed," his father was saying next, as if Billy had not guessed. "Mr. Franklin has never been too busy to be concerned for thy future."

Billy bent down and pulled up a weed, which he studied thoughtfully.

"Thee sees, son, it is not as if thee were any ordinary young man. Nor is it because thee is my son. Both Mr. Collinson and Mr. Franklin have called thee ingenious. The question is, what is thee going to do with that ingenuity? The Creator did not grant it to thee to be set aside."

"I have just been to the river looking for specimens," Billy volunteered, before he remembered that this was not where he was supposed to have spent the afternoon.

"And found no new ones," his father continued for him, choosing to overlook his admission. "Thee has already seen for thyself that every animal, like every plant, endeavors to live where it can best survive. It is logical and sensible that only a certain few of all the numbers there are find Kingses-

sing the best environment in which to fulfill their require-
ments for living and the successful perpetuation of their
species."

Billy had heard this before, but still he listened atten-
tively, because in this principle lay, he believed, the answer
to one of the still incompletely explored riddles of life on
earth.

"In Connecticut," John Bartram went on, after a pause
and a long look at the pensive boy, "there must be a quantity
of other varieties. Mr. Franklin has a friend there, the
Reverend Mr. Jared Eliot. I myself have had considerable
correspondence with him. Although I had hoped to be able
to journey to Carolina to renew my acquaintance with Dr.
Garden in Charleston, the mischievous Indians have become
so treacherous that it is no longer safe to trust them, even in
their greatest pretense of friendship." His face darkened, and
he turned away with a brooding look.

"Mr. Collinson is also concerned, up to a point, with the
encroachment of our savage foes," John mused aloud, staring
at the cypress as though speaking to it. "He recently wrote
that he hoped his old friend would not expose himself to
Indian cruelties. In the next sentence he requested a dozen
boxes of new seeds. New seeds, indeed! Does he suppose I
can manufacture them?"

"The Reverend Mr. Eliot?" prompted Billy hopefully.

"I have little heart or relish to travel now," his father pro-
ceded in his dismal vein, "not to Dr. Garden's, or to Dr.
Colden's, or even to Dr. Mitchell's in Virginia. Nevertheless,
I replied to Peter that I would set out again, and if I died a
martyr to botany, then God's will be done!"

He turned from the tree and peered off as if to see, rising
beyond the river, a whole new wilderness to be explored.
"Connecticut might still be possible. It is a part of the world
I have not yet traveled in, and I believe the journey is not
too difficult, although I fear there are dangerous rattlesnakes

in the gloomy precipices. We may be exposed to horrid circumstances in passing across rivers and climbing over mountains. And thee understands that we shall be obliged to
follow the tracks of wild beasts as our only guides through
these desolate thickets.

"Still, I think we must go whilst we can still go anywhere.
Mr. Franklin says he will write to Mr. Eliot. I fear he will
overpraise me; he has some nonsense in mind about a twenty-
page folio of large paper well filled. I trust that the Reverend Mr. Eliot will not be disappointed."

John Bartram looked back to his slender son, already taller
than his father, with his bright expectant eyes fixed so
steadily upon him. "Even so, my Billy, I find it most unlikely
that he could be anything save pleased with thee."

CHAPTER 2

THE GARDEN

"If you would be happy for a week, take a wife;
If you would be happy for a month, kill your pig;
But if you would be happy all your life, plant a garden."

Old Chinese Proverb

Billy Bartram stood at the deep, uncurtained window of his father's study and watched the rain falling into the garden. Beyond the garden, the river, although only about one hundred and fifty yards away, lay almost completely obscured in mist.

The grayness of the morning matched Billy's mood. Until then he had been impatient for this day to arrive. Now, stiffly dressed in his best traveling clothes and looking out at the dripping trees, he found it difficult to understand how he could have been so anxious to leave.

This, he realized with regret, was a typical reaction of his. So many times before, he had been eager for some kind of change and then, when the change had come, been reluctant to accept it. He saw this tendency of wavering as an indication of weakness, and he sensed that it was a real disappointment to his father, who was so strong and practical and wise.

After all, he reasoned, standing there at the window around which his father had carved by hand a tracery like the folds of linen, it was not as though he were going to a strange place to be among strangers. He was on his way to North Carolina to stay with his Uncle William, whom he had visited before. He would see his cousin Mary, who had surprisingly shared his interest in wild flowers and birds—in fact, all animals—and had understood his need to draw them. And was he not still the same Billy Bartram who had loved nothing better than journeying?

The difference was that before this he had always known that he was coming home. Now it had been decided that he must remain at Cape Fear and make his living as a trader. He felt his eyes start to burn.

"Dear God," he murmured, "I am twenty-two years old. Pray do not let me disgrace my father and myself by behaving like a homesick child."

It had been six years since Billy and his father had made the journey to Connecticut to visit Jared Eliot, a journey which, as it turned out, had not been as fraught with peril as John Bartram had feared. It was typical of his father, Billy thought with a faint smile, to overemphasize possible dangers, particularly those concerning encounters with Indians or snakes. And yet his father was by nature sanguine and optimistic, far more so than his troubled son.

During those six years, Billy had continued to occupy himself with his drawings. Some of the first of these he had sent to Jane Colden, and had received from her long letters of encouragement and praise. "I can teach you no more," she had written. "You have already surpassed me in skill and imagination."

Peter Collinson had also praised Billy's ingenuity. Across the ocean, as carefully wrapped as his father's seeds and roots, went Billy's drawings of leaves and turtles. Some of the turtle drawings had even been published in British magazines. And for the English ornithologist, George Edwards, Billy had shot and dried specimens of Pennsylvania birds and sent them along with their descriptions. From these skins, prepared by his "obliging friend," Edwards had made some of the first American bird drawings ever seen across the Atlantic.

But Billy's life had not been concerned alone with the delights of the woods and fields and river. For a while his father had sent him as an apprentice to Captain Child, a merchant in Philadelphia. John Bartram could not be convinced that his artistic son was not leading a life of idleness. If Billy could not, or would not, become a physician, a printer, or a surveyor, he might at least learn the practice of keeping a store.

Billy had failed even in this. As it had in the schoolroom, his attention wandered to the open windows; even in the city he was continually diverted by the out-of-doors. Furthermore, however diligently he tried, he could not seem to master the setting down of figures, and the adding and subtracting of them. Numbers remained a mystery to him. Yet he could count the petals of a flower or the feathers on a bird's wing with no difficulty at all.

Just then there came the sound of running footsteps in the hall, and into the study burst Elizabeth, his twin sister. "Oh, Billy," and she thrust her damp cheek against his, "how we shall miss thee!"

Billy hugged her and then held her away from him and studied her. In her narrow delicate face, with her long, finely chiseled nose and wide-set eyes, and her thin yet gentle mouth, he saw a reflection of himself. Her tears made him feel braver. "There is no need for crying," he told her more sternly than he had intended. "I am not going to die."

"But thee is going away forever," she said, as if it were the same thing.

Billy knew why he was being sent away. He had tried a variety of jobs at home and failed.

Although Captain Child and his wife claimed that they loved Billy as a son, they could no longer afford to provide even his lodging. Through his carelessness in keeping accounts and his trusting attitude toward strangers, he had cost them too much already. Yet Mrs. Child had wept as she watched Billy pack his few belongings, and the captain had turned away his face.

Elizabeth, seeing her twin's sad expression, attempted to be cheerful. "Thee will do well down there. We all believe it." 'I have never done well anywhere,' Billy was thinking. 'How can my family be so confident?' His sister was holding out to him something that she had brought with her and had been awkwardly clutching all this time. It was a leather case and inside was a tablet of paper and a quill. "So that thee will write to us often, Billy. Oh, I pray thee does. Then thee won't seem so far away."

Billy took the case and thanked his sister, but he was not especially happy with his present. Letter writing had always been a chore for him; he had written very few. Now and then he corresponded with Mr. Collinson in London; he had written to Mr. Edwards and Miss Jane Colden, and occasionally to his cousin Mary; that was about all. Proper sentences were tedious to construct, and spelling was to him, as it was to his father, an obscure art. He felt that what he set down on paper made him appear even less intelligent than he was.

Drawing was different; he seemed at his best then. Nevertheless, reluctantly he promised Elizabeth that he would write.

The rain was splashing out of the watering trough onto the path by the southeast corner of the house. Billy's father had hewn the trough from a solid boulder, just as he had built his house from hewn stone quarried in his fields. To Jared Eliot, he described how he split rocks seventeen feet long, fashioned steps and sills, and decorated window frames with ornamental scrolls. On one gray panel he inscribed: "John : Ann : Bartram : 1731." The fame of the house crossed the ocean; Peter Collinson praised his "great art and industry in building it."

But it was in his garden that John Bartram took his greatest pride. From the day in 1728 when at twenty-nine he had bought the land on the west bank of the Schuylkill River at Sheriff Owen Owen's sale, farming and then botany had been his chief delight.

He was not alone. Ever since William Penn arrived in the New World with a charter from Charles II and a wish to set out a garden, early inhabitants had been busy planting. And before that, Penn had urged the settlers to plan their houses "so that there may be grounds on each side, for Gardens, or Orchards, or fields." He never failed to stress the desirability of "studying and following nature and endeavoring to become good naturalists."

For himself, Penn selected 6,500 acres on the river, which in 1685 he began to develop into an estate of unprecedented elegance, with a mansion, many roads, and varied and extensive gardens presided over by no less than five gardeners imported from England, along with most of the plants. Lawns were sown with English grass seed. Grapevines for his vineyard were ordered from France; full-sized trees were moved from Virginia and Maryland.

In the spring of 1701, the founder of Pennsylvania moved into Pennsbury Manor, at that time the uncontested pride of the colony. John Bartram, living not far away, was two years old.

Inspired partly by Penn and partly by the wealth of new plants in a strange country, other settlers planned ambitious gardens. Penn's own secretary, a Scotch-Irish merchant named James Logan, came to Philadelphia with him in 1699, at the age of twenty-five. Outside of the city, which was then only a cross-hatching of streets and a few brick buildings, he acquired the plantation of Stenton. Upon its five hundred acres, he had constructed in 1728 a stately Georgian house with paneled walls and wide staircases, where he entertained both nobles and Indians. An avenue of fine hemlocks led to the front door.

Two rooms on the second floor were one day to hold the colony's most impressive library: Logan's collection of several thousand volumes, including the works of Euclid, Ptolemy, and Archimedes, which John Bartram, Dr. Christopher Witt, Francis Daniel Pastorius, and Benjamin Franklin borrowed and read.

Dr. Witt was an Englishman who arrived in the New World in 1704 and became a neighbor of James Logan's. A physician, clockmaker, musician, and Rosicrucian mystic, he also established one of the first true botanical gardens in America. As a practicing doctor, he was particularly interested in herbs and their curative powers. When he met John Bartram in 1736, he encouraged the farmer of Kingsessing to study plants for their medicinal values.

John did not have to be encouraged. Medicine had fascinated him for a long time. Years later Billy was to write of him that it was this fascination with the curing properties of plants that had led him from simple farming into botany. His father, he explained, "had a very early inclination to the study of physic and surgery. He even acquired so much knowledge in the practice of the latter science as to be useful; in many instances he gave relief to his poor neighbors."

John, though, insisted that ever since he was ten years old he had had "a great inclination to plants." Actually he was a very good farmer, using his own sensible conservation methods of fertilizing with natural materials, mulching, and rotating crops: hay for the animals, wheat for flour, and flax for weaving. In all, he farmed about two hundred and fifty highly fertile acres.

John's first wife, Mary, had worried about her husband's new preoccupation with botanizing. It did not seem to her that he could possibly support a family with the practice of science. The microscope and telescope which Mr. Logan taught him to use could not be expected to take the place of the plow, even in the Bartrams' simple Quaker frugality. Yet it was John who said, "It is through the telescope I see God in his glory."

James Logan was quick to urge John to continue his scientific pursuits. As early as 1729 he had written to England to obtain a copy of John Parkinson's *Paradisi in Sole Paradisus Terrestris,* a tome which contained the subtitle: "A Garden of all Sorts of Pleasant Flowers Which Our English Ayre will Permitt to be noursed up: with a Kitchen garden, etc." The book had been published in London in 1656. William Penn's secretary, who was to become the mayor of Philadelphia and then chief justice and acting governor of Pennsylvania, wanted the herbal as a present for his young acquaintance "worthy of a heavier purse than fortune has yet allowed him." He had, Logan went on, "a genius perfectly well turned for botany."

Logan himself had been experimenting with Indian maize and the spreading of pollen, in an effort to prove the new theory that there were sexual differences in plants. When he heard that John had traveled to Philadelphia to buy botanical books and a Latin grammar to enable him to read them, Logan offered him any of his own books that he might desire. He introduced him to the binomial naming system of Linnaeus, helping him with the unfamiliar Latin taxonomy and little dreaming that one day the same Linnaeus would name this untutored farmer the greatest practical botanist of his age.

Logan's neighbor, Dr. Witt, had a remarkable library of his own. As John Bartram wrote to Peter Collinson, it "was furnished with books containing different kinds of learning . . . as Philosophy, Natural Magic, Divinity, nay even Mystic Divinity; all of which were subjects of our discourse within doors."

John's scientific mind had to reject the magic and mysticism, but the rejection was managed with his characteristic tact. "I handle these fancies with more tenderness with him than I should with many others, thee knows," he went on to Collinson, "because I respect the man. He hath a considerable share of good in him . . . and hath attained the greatest knowledge in botany of any I have discoursed with."

Pastorius and Joseph Breintnall, cloth agent for Collinson in the New World and a friend of Franklin's, whom Franklin once described as a "great lover of poetry, reading all that he could meet with and writing some that was tolerable," also made available their volumes. It is reported that Breintnall's sending of Bartram's botanical diaries to Collinson began their long and memorable exchange.

This more or less informal lending and borrowing of books was bound to lead to the establishment of a local library. It was Franklin who first proposed it in 1730, and he chose Breintnall as its secretary and Logan to give advice in the selection of books. The books must largely be obtained from the Old World, mostly from London, and so it was that Peter Collinson, with his interest in science, was offered, and accepted, the position of agent for the library.

Among the first volumes he sent to the new Library Company of Philadelphia were the works of Ovid, Virgil, and Seneca; Addison, Milton, and Pope; Sterne and Swift. As his own particular contribution, and as the library's first gift, he included Philip Miller's *The Gardener's Dictionary*, published in 1731 and the standard authority of the time. A friend of Collinson's, Miller had succeeded his father as superintendent of the famous Physic Gardens at Chelsea, a position he held for fifty years. His *Dictionary* was called the foundation of horticultural knowledge in Europe, and as such was praised by Linnaeus.

The eighth Lord Petre, Bartram's first patron, sent John a copy in which John inscribed: "John Bartram His Booke 1739 A Present from ye Right Honorable Lord Petre."

That farmer, though, that father of a rapidly growing family, that simple plant collector, could hardly afford to join the new company around which the intellectual life of the colony had begun to revolve. He spoke with some longing to his friend Ben of the literary treasures just beyond his reach. At their next meeting the library directors passed a resolution: "As Mr. John Bartram is a deserving man, he should have free access to the Library, and be permitted to read and borrow books."

Peter Collinson, the London agent for the Library Company for almost thirty years, continued to include whatever books on the subjects of botany and horticulture he could find, and these were particularly welcomed by the Philadelphia members. Why had gardening become so tremendously popular in the new colony?

The settlers, for the most part, were British, and Englishmen had always been gardeners. For one thing, the generally temperate climate and especially the abundance of rainfall encouraged plants to grow. For another, many cities were in deplorable conditions, overrun with vermin or plagues, with garbage and other refuse piled in the streets. There was thieving and looting, and appalling odor and disease. Men of any means, whenever and wherever possible, escaped to the country.

Thomas Fuller wrote that gardening "crept out of Holland" and into Kent during the reign of Elizabeth. William III, coming from Holland, set the style for the planting of formal flower beds in the flamboyant and colorful Dutch manner.

Lords and ladies spared no expense to lay out gardens the size of parks. Lord Petre imported trees and shrubs from the New World; so did the Dukes of Richmond, Norfolk, Bedford, Argyll, and Marlborough. Lord Petre is said to have planted thousands of trees, many of them cedars. Most of the evergreens native to England then were dwarfed and low, like the juniper and the yew.

But the joys of horticulture did not belong solely to the nobility. Busy Peter Collinson spent hours planting and transplanting, collecting camellais, magnolias, and orange and lemon trees, exotic species rare in Britain.

Actually it has been recorded that oranges did grow in England in the sixteenth century. Sir Francis Carew is said to have planted them at his home in Surrey. By the next hundred years, inspired perhaps by the fashions in France, several Englishmen of wealth had built their own orangeries, stocked with young trees from Italy and Spain. But the great freeze of 1740 put a temporary end to the growing of citrus in Britain.

Like John Bartram, Collinson was also interested in the medicinal qualities of quinine and other herbs and corresponded with botanists all over the world. When Linnaeus asked him for a catalogue of his garden, Collinson dutifully sent one, but characteristically could not resist adding, "You must remember that I am a merchant, a man of great business with many affairs in my head and on my hands."

It was, on the whole, a propitious time for John Bartram. Noblemen with their new and vast landscape parks longed for different and exotic plants with which to embellish them. Peter Collinson had wasted not a moment in instructing them in the setting out of their trees: "To know how to mix them in planting is another manner of painting with living pencils."

As in all ages, competition ran rampant. Thoughts turned hopefully to the New World, whose vegetation had already been praised by Raleigh, Catesby, Penn, Franklin, and others. Might it not be possible that American plants could grow in English gardens?

Collinson believed that it was indeed possible. And until the Revolution put an end to transatlantic traffic, plants from North America traveled on almost every ship that sailed from the Delaware River. The mountain laurel named for Peter Kalm, bush honeysuckles, rhododendrons, maples, spruce, and hemlocks—all found their way to English landscape parks, where they prospered in the temperate climate. American gentians and ferns and asters flourished in English garden borders. John Bartram could keep them supplied from his apparently limitless wilderness if, as Collinson had to keep reminding the landowners, they would remember to meet their payments on time.

By 1775, whatever was popular in England was beginning to be in demand on the Continent. This was in the nature of a reversal, since formerly it had been France, Italy, and the Low Countries that set the fashions. Now, all at once, *le jardin anglais* was in style as far away as Russia. Perhaps due to Capability Brown's influence, the landscape park was imitated far and wide. With the assistance of Franklin and others, John Bartram's American plants spread from country to country, and his mark, if not yet his name, was frequently seen.

In a period when science was regarded as a suitable subject for poetry, Dr. Erasmus Darwin wrote:

> *What beaux and beauties crowd the gaudy groves*
> *And woo and win their vegetable loves.*

As a footnote to this, he added that Linnaeus had already demonstrated that "all flowers contain families of males or females, or both; and on their marriages he constructed his invaluable system of Botany."

Actually, the eighteenth century marked the beginning of the time when plants were seen whole and their functions studied. The medieval concept of nature as a mysterious and forbidden source of study was turned about; now the ways of God and the ways of nature became the same, and both were considered the ways of reason.

How different John Bartram's own garden, with its straight parallel paths, stone steps and terraces, and its well-filled, well-tended flower beds, was from the landscape parks that he supplied. And yet, it had a wildness and a weediness that the followers of the naturalistic movement would have admired. In his vast and expanding curiosity about everything that grew, Bartram collected, planted, and transplanted a wide variety of specimens. Saddlebags that he unpacked after his collecting journeys contained roots, seeds, and switches that were sorted and stored or else set out at once.

The Quaker plowman believed the specimens he sought and discovered in the wilderness would thrive best under similar conditions at home, and so many of the most prized locations in his beloved garden were rocky tangles and untidy hedgerows.

Built into his chimney, beside his large fireplace, were special warming closets or cupboards for the drying of plants and seeds, to prevent mildew and sprouting on their long journeys. Many of the seeds were prepared for their overseas travels in a special potting shed which he built toward the north of his house shortly after he began shipping seeds abroad. There, in the hand-hewn shed at the end of the grape arbor, he packed in silk bags and then in boxes the samples of wild flowers, shrubs, and trees that were to cross the ocean and blossom in gardens he would never see.

Peter Collinson wrote out minute instructions for the packing and shipping of specimens. The loss of a packet of seeds, he once said, distressed him far more than the loss of a prime minister. Boxes in the stormy winter months, he suggested, should be stowed safely beneath the captain's bunk and securely slatted and lathed against raids by the captain's cat.

There also, in his potting shed, he unpacked the bulbs that he received from England in partial exchange for the seeds he sent: crocuses, tulips—wildly popular in Britain during and since William and Mary's reign—narcissus, irises, lilies, and gladioli, which he planted in his beds sloping down to the river's edge and watered from his boulder trough.

Of the double narcissus which Collinson included in one shipment, Bartram wrote that there were already too many of these in Pennsylvania gardens. Early settlers had carried the bulbs with them when they left their English homes, and they had planted them wherever they built their houses.

The simple planting and growing of exotic species, though, whether for variety or collections, was not the aim of men like Bartram and Collinson. They were botanists first of all, and, like others in this age of scientific awakening, they studied their plants and sought to spread their botanical knowledge. Classifiers were anxious to name new plants. Linnaeus of Uppsala, Gronovius of Leiden, and Dillenius of Oxford were only a few of the taxonomists who rejoiced that John Bartram had opened up another continent for them, and they wrote to tell him so.

But perhaps the most discerning and descriptive tribute to Bartram's work lies in a letter written by Dr. Garden to Dr. Colden in 1754 after a visit to Kingsessing. "His garden is a perfect portraiture of himself. Here you meet with a row of rare plants almost covered over with weeds, here with a

Beautiful Shrub even Luxuriant amongst the Briars, and in another corner an Elegant and Lofty tree lost in a common thicket. On our way from town to his house he carried me to several rocks and Dens where he shewed me some of his rare plants, which he brought from the Mountains, &c. In a word he disclaims to have a garden less than Pennsylvania & Every den is an Arbour, Every run of water, a Canal, & every small level Spot a Parterre, where he nurses up some of his Idol Flowers & cultivates his darling productions."

Dr. Garden went on to praise his new friend's "ease, Gaiety & happy Alacrity," adding that Bartram then invited his company to dine "with so much rural vivacity that everyone were agreeably pleased and surprised."

It was no wonder that Billy would miss his father's home.

The father just then came into the room where Billy still stood watching the rain spatter from the long wooden well sweep and onto the drenched path. The boxbushes glistened. Tree trunks gleamed black against the gray and green background.

"So, Billy, here thee is," John Bartram said briskly. "The carriage will soon be ready." And then he quietly closed the doors of the room.

Billy prepared for a brief and final lecture. He turned from the window and faced his father gravely.

"I suppose," John began, "that thee has packed thy Bible. I hope that thee will also carry thy small book of psalms in thy pocket. They will enhance thy idle moments. Oh, Billy, love God! Fear and adore him."

Billy was not startled to hear this. How often had his father exhorted all his children to love God and one another! He nodded, waiting.

"I have copied for thee the advice printed by Mr. Franklin in that same issue of his *Almanack* in which he published my essay concerning the use of red cedar for fencing, calling it 'of more service to the publick than three hundred and seventy-five prefaces of his own writing.'"

Billy smiled. He had also heard this before. His father proceeded to read:

"First, Let the Fear of HIM who form'd thy Frame,
Whose Hand sustain'd thee e'er thou hads't a Name,
Who brought thee into Birth, with Pow'r of Thought
Receptive of immortal Good, be wrought
Deep in thy Soul. His, not thy own, thou art;
To him resign the Empire of thy Heart."

John Bartram handed the paper to his son, who inserted it in his writing case.

John went on: "Thee is about to embark not only upon a new journey, but also upon a new life. Thee will be far away, it is true, but not amongst strangers nor in a strange place. Honor and revere thy relatives as thee has thy parents; regard and benefit everyone when it is in thy power.

"In the south," he mused in a faraway tone, "I have found that customs differ from ours. In Virginia, and farther still, men are more particular about their manners. Colonel Custis and Mr. William Byrd, as well as Mr. Collinson, impressed this upon me. Did I tell thee," he went on, digressing, "that Colonel Custis's daughter-in-law has married for the second time, a Colonel Washington? I met him once in Williamsburg. He seems a person of considerable elegance, sending to London for all that he wears and constantly increasing his estate called Mount Vernon, most pleasantly situated on the Potomac River. I understand that he is experimenting with the grafting of fruit trees."

He continued: "Colonel Custis has what I consider the finest collection of lilacs in America, and I so informed Collinson. Billy, we must work to improve the strain of our lilacs here." He appeared to have forgotten for the moment that his son was leaving Pennsylvania.

"Father," Billy began tentatively, but his son's voice reminded John Bartram that he had more to say. "Remember another maxim Mr. Franklin has taught: 'Lost time is never found again.' Hours spent in daydreaming are hours cast away. Be diligent, and squander time no more than thee would squander gold. Be friendly to all, but avoid the society of those who are irreligious or immoral. Thee will find these even in the simplicity of Cape Fear. Yet never fail to render assistance if thee can to any of whatever sort who appear in distress or need."

Billy sighed. Who knew into what company he might fall? Already he had proved to be a poor judge of character, trusting thieves, granting credit to the lazy and shiftless. It had been one of the reasons why he had been unable to keep his jobs. Every man he met had seemed to have good qualities; it was difficult if not impossible to distinguish between the honest and the dishonest until it was too late.

John sighed too; he knew his son's weakness. And yet he was a good boy, by nature the best of the lot. He had not rushed away to sea like his brother Moses, to end up "trembling and tumbling about the world," as Collinson had written in despair. He was, as his father liked to say, his "little botanist."

And yet, on the other hand, Billy totally lacked the dependability of his younger brother John. Now, with Billy going away to North Carolina to live, it was more than likely that young John would inherit all the farm, including his beloved garden. At sixty-two, which his father felt was an advanced age, such things were much on his mind.

He turned back to his son, who was standing respectfully silent, turning the leather case in his hand. No doubt he was already planning the drawings that he would make. "I need not remind thee to be honorable in all things and at all times, for thee has never been otherwise, but I must impress upon thee the need for frugality. It seems a virtue thee has had difficulty to learn, although thee has had every example in thy home. Generosity and charity are excellent virtues in their place; yet I fear thee is overly liberal with thy funds."

Billy, who had few funds and had often seen what little he owned slip through his fingers, nodded with a rueful smile, wondering what else his father would think of to say to him. He could hear the horses on the cart road.

"Respect the honor of women upon all occasions. Speak well of them, or speak not at all. Also, never forget to be on thy guard against lurking rattlesnakes and barbarous Indians, and put none of thy trust in either." And as Billy still smiled, receiving this familiar admonition, his father, who had started away on hearing the horses, came back and laid his hand on his son's sleeve. "I shall not cease to pray for thy safety on thy journey and in thy profession, whatever it may turn out to be. Pray daily thyself, that thee may be kept from evil. And Billy, love and fear God, and walk humbly before him."

The two men faced one another for a moment, then both looked away, out of the window toward the rain-masked river. And Harvey, John's servant and steward, knocked on the door to announce the arrival of the carriage.

CHAPTER 3

"THE CAPE OF FEARE"

"Dost thou love life? Then do not squander
time, for that is the stuff life is made of."
Benjamin Franklin

The name of the cape came from the shoals beneath the roiled surface of the Atlantic. Inland, the Carolina river began by winding gently through tree-lined meadows, much as the Schuylkill flowed past Kingsessing. Where the low country became tidewater marsh, the current moved sluggishly against the tall grasses where wrens built their nests in the rushes and cattails, and raccoon and rail hunted, and flocks of redwinged blackbirds fluttered and then dropped like nets over the reeds.

Where the fresh-water river became salt, an estuary formed, protected from the sea by a long, narrow sandspit. As the current pushed the sand along and brought with it fine silt from the upland meadows, an underwater shoal was formed, stretching twenty miles south from the estuary. Because of its shape, where it rose glistening, this shoal on its long "handle" was described as the Frying Pan. And because of the shoal's unexpected treachery and danger, the headland rising above it was called Cape Fear.

The treachery and danger lay in the assault of the seas' constant battering. Upon the submerged and emerged barriers alike, huge waves exploded. Hurricanes wreaked their violence. And all the while the river, pouring its flood downstream, carved channels where there had been none before and piled up silt to block to old ones.

In 1585 an Englishman named John White was sailing from his native land to that barely known island off the coast called Roanoke. An artist of some repute, he had come to paint the New World. In a sudden storm his ship was swept so close to the sandspit that, in his terror, he christened the place *Promontorium Tremendum.* That very year, Sir Richard Grenville, leader of Sir Walter Raleigh's first expedition, also had a narrow escape on the shoal. He was, he recorded in his log, "in great danger of a wracke on a beach called the Cape of Feare." He had apparently heard of White's name for it and deemed it fitting.

Less than a hundred years later, another Briton, a planter living on the island of Barbados, set sail for the Carolina coast in search of more land for crops. His name was William Hilton, and on October 12, 1663, his ship, the *Adventure,* dropped anchor off the headland his men then called Cape Fair. After their stormy voyage, it is little wonder that the land and the broad river appeared fair to them.

Hilton gave to his fellow planters in Barbados and Bermuda a rosy report of what he found. Not only was the land suitable for planting, but there were also high meadows for buildings and pastures, and, along the waterways, forests that lined each bank. He had seen majestic oaks for timber. Piney woods would provide boards for houses and spars for ships. The woods also appeared to be the haunt of wild turkey and deer and "great flocks of Parakeeto's." Duck, curlew, and other game was abundant.

Perhaps most advantageous of all was the fact that the Indians were friendly. The chief, indeed, was so friendly that he made William Hilton a present of "two very handsome proper young Indian women." The gift, though, turned out to be an embarrassment to the captain, since the girls proved so anxious to please him that he encountered some difficulty in freeing himself from their attentions.

But the report was favorable, and the river was settled. Called the Sapona for the Indians the Barbadians found there, it was later named for King Charles II, and after that known for a while as the Clarendon. Lumber was cut, turpentine and pitch were barreled, and the planks and barrels were carried up the river on piraguas—canoelike boats hollowed from cypress trunks, sometimes with a flat bottom and decks at either end, and often with a mast and sail. These "periaugers," as they were locally called, were rowed in deep water and poled across the shallows. Where the current was swift, they were pulled by ropes from the bridle paths on shore. In a favoring wind the boats sailed freely. Even so, the winding thirty-mile trip from Wilmington on the Lower Cape Fear to Bladen Court House on the site of the present Elizabethtown took far longer by water than by land.

Little by little, as the river traffic increased, families from the Lower Cape moved inland toward Court House Landing. Records say that an Englishman, John Baptista Ashe, owned a large plantation there on the sixty-foot-high west bank of the Cape Fear River. At his death, "Ashwood" was acquired by William Bartram, the younger half brother of John and the uncle of Billy.

John and William's father, also named William, had moved to North Carolina around 1709, shortly after his second marriage. Elizabeth was a popular name in those days: both of William's wives were Elizabeths.

It has been suggested that the reason he left his Darby, Pennsylvania, home was that he was in trouble with the

Darby Friends Meeting. All the Bartrams were independent and original thinkers, and they expressed their opinions freely. Many times their observations, particularly in the field of science, did not meet with the approval of their fellow Quakers. John himself fell into disfavor with the Friends, yet he never renounced his membership in the Society, and he continued to attend Meeting.

On the Cape Fear River, John's half brother, William Bartram, brought up his children—Billy, Sarah, and Mary—in the great house he built on a bluff above the water at Donaho's Creek. Bladen Court House was the seat of Bladen Precinct, and boats were constantly moving upstream from Wilmington and downstream from Cross Creek, which after the Revolution became known as Fayetteville. When Billy Bartram of Kingsessing first went to visit his uncle and cousins in 1757, he found the upriver towns sleepy and undisturbed—a few pine cabins surrounded by live oaks draped in Spanish moss, with dogs and chickens scratching in the sandy soil around the dooryards where crape myrtles bloomed and rabbit tobacco ran wild.

Down by the water's edge, bald cypresses stood with their buttressed trunks and their gnarled "knees" rising around them. Willows trailed their branches in the slow-moving stream, and jessamine and honeysuckle wreathed the steep limestone bank.

It had been easy in those days to fall in love with the gentle southern scene. Sometimes Billy had sat for hours by the silty river, drawing the herons that came to feed, or the turtles that floated by, sunning on logs, or the indolent fish that tilted like flakes of gold through the sunlit shallows. Sometimes he had gone hunting wild turkey in the pine barrens with his Uncle William and laughed to hear him call the cock by imitating its gobble, while far away in the trees a little brown sparrow piped a plaintive song. Sometimes he had lain in bed late, listening to the redbirds and mockingbirds that never ceased their singing, and other days he had risen early to seek in the tidal mudflats the tracks of otter and egret and rail.

But that carefree, dreamlike visit had been four years ago. Now Billy was here to prosper in business, or at least that was what his father and uncle prayerfully hoped. John had financed the setting-up of a shop for him and sent his usual words of wisdom: "My dear child, I have no advice to give thee but to remember thee of my former general instructions: fear God and walk humbly before him; practice all virtues and eschew all vice; take care of being beguiled by vain recreations . . . but keep close to industry, temperance, and frugality; thee hath left a good character behind in town; pray don't forget it . . . I have thy welfare much at heart."

His Uncle William had introduced his many Quaker and Scottish friends also living in close communities on the Northwest Branch, and they promised to come and buy. It was a propitious beginning; it seemed as though at last "poor Billy," as he had come to be known, would have his long-awaited success.

Billy himself had many doubts. He simply could not imagine himself as a trader. Business was business, and it would be the same at Cape Fear as it had been in Philadelphia. Prospective customers would come, and they would enjoy conversation with the polite, intelligent young man, but they were more apt than not to leave without buying. No selected items were eagerly pushed before them; no bargains were hopefully pointed out.

The sad truth was that Billy did not really care whether they bought or not. Figures were still the same as they had been before, next to impossible to fathom. People were the same too; he enjoyed their company. But in spite of his previous unfortunate experiences and his father's ready advice, he could not learn to pick the honest from the dishonest. He still befriended tramps and trusted thieves.

If this were the worst, it could have been forgiven. There were others who could not add and subtract, or distinguish fraud. What really disturbed Billy's friends and family was his tendency to close the store and wander off into the woods, or spend the afternoon along the riverbank. Sometimes he would walk all the way to his uncle's lake at the White Marsh, where Colonel Bartram had his mill. Sometimes he would follow a new bird for hours through the deep, vine-covered ravine behind the main street of the town.

Understandably, Captain and Mrs. Child's city shop had seemed a prison to a boy who yearned to be roaming the countryside hunting for plants or looking at birds; but for a man of twenty-two, fortunate enough to have been set up in a shop of his own, to be so irresponsible and careless was a source not only of grief but also of mystery.

One evening at the supper table, Billy's Uncle William, observing what was happening and at a loss to know how to explain it to the parents in Kingsessing, made one further attempt to discourage his nephew's wanderings. "Billy," he began, leaning forward earnestly, "isn't thee frightened when thee walks so far into the woods? The country is more settled, to be sure, than it was when thee was here last, but there are still wild places where venomous snakes and even hostile Indians abound."

This sounded so much like what he had heard at home that Billy had to smile. "My own father warned me in the same vein. Yet I wonder how much heed he pays to his own advice. I have heard him tell about holding out his hat for a rattlesnake to strike, and then admit that with death the splendor of its skin diminishes." He paused, and his face clouded. "Still, Indians are a different matter. For some reason my father has a general dread of them."

His uncle's face also clouded and he looked down at his empty plate. A slave, Lonzo, promptly refilled it, but William did not eat. Mary, sitting across from Billy, stretched out her foot under the table and touched her cousin's ankle.

Billy mistook this for an accident and blushed. "In truth, Uncle William," he plunged on precipitously, "I have been surprised by my father's unreasonable fears. One time, in his journeying far beyond the mountains, he met an Indian chief who snatched off his hat in great passion and chewed it all around the brim. My father said this was a certain warning that the chief might kill him or any other white man he encountered. I have even heard him tell Mr. Franklin that he would like to see all Indians driven back a thousand miles into the wilderness, for they will never love us nor keep peace long with us."

His uncle was looking graver than ever. Mary was frowning and shaking her head. Billy had just about decided that he had said enough when he remembered something else. "Once at an Indian council, where my father was made welcome, having been sent by Mr. Logan in hope of arranging a peace, some of the men gathered there were discussing the rolling of stones down a hillside to produce rain. My father, as usual, scoffed at the superstition, and in proof of what he said sent a few rocks down the slope. When a day or two later it chanced to rain, the chief declared that Father was to blame."

Lonzo passed him a dish containing a pilau of rice and shrimp baked by Old Cloe. Thin though he was, Billy ate as much as any man. He helped himself again. "At that same council meeting," he went on, as if mechanically wound up, "when they lay sleeping on the ground, my father was awakened by a noise, a cry of beast or bird he did not recognize. He called out to inquire what it might be. The chief, believing him afeared, shouted back, 'Lie still, John.' My father told me afterward that he had never heard him speak so much plain English."

"Billy," his uncle said, turning his grave expression full upon him, "that will be sufficient about Indians."

The sun, the next few days, burned with such a brightness on every damp leaf and petal as to make them look enameled. Unknown birds called from every thicket. It was June, and the air was heavy with musky magnolia and honey locust. To Billy it had never seemed more difficult, if not impossible, to remain in the shop. One morning his cousin Mary took pity on him.

She appeared suddenly in the open doorway of the store. Light fell glistening on her long hair and on her arms, over one of which hung a basket. "Billy," she almost whispered, though there was no one else there, no would-be buyers or borrowers, "close up the shop. I have some lunch for us here in the hamper—wild-pigeon pie and rabbit. Little Cloe packed it. The horses are ready. Let us ride far away into the country or along the river. Soon it may be too unseasonable to go."

Billy bent over his drawing of a green heron and appeared to find something wrong with its beak which needed immediate correction. "What would Uncle William say," he finally managed, "if we took the horses?" What he was really thinking was: 'What would Uncle William say if I closed the store again?'

Mary laughed. "Silly Billy! Does thee imagine that I would take the horses without Father's permission? Thee may not believe this, but it was he who suggested it. He said thee was not as hearty as thee had been and he feared thee was homesick for thy father's garden. Is it true, Billy? Is thee homesick?"

Billy stared at his cousin and hardly knew what to say. She looked so hopeful, standing there with the basket on her arm. She seemed so innocent and untouched, as if she could not bear to be hurt. She was lovely, and he loved her very much. "It would be strange, would it not," he said with some difficulty, "were I not to miss my family?"

For just a moment he had forgotten that she was his family too. He had a sudden vision of his twin sister, Elizabeth, waiting where Mary waited. Then the vision faded and his delicate face and expressive eyes brightened. "I need not be asked more than once to lock this door. Come, hurry, before thy father changes his mind or a customer approaches!"

They rode, on that enchanted day, across rolling farmland and through upland woods. Billy had a hard time containing his exuberance. When they finally dismounted by a bridge across a narrow creek, Billy ran to his cousin and hugged her.

They sat side by side on the bridge, swinging their legs over the edge, dropping bits of willow and bay twigs into the stream. Tall, slender trees—turkey oaks, sweet gums, chinquapins, and loblolly pines—grew near the water's edge, rising close and straight up like a curtain, while high overhead the sun beat down. Muskrats played among the submerged grasses. Dragonflies like the ones on the Schuylkill hovered over the flowering arrowhead and cow lilies.

Mary let her head rest on Billy's shoulder. He felt the softness of her hair on his bare throat. His eye fell on the hamper, and for the first time in his life he decided that he was not hungry.

A pair of phoebes, also like the ones on the Schuylkill, waited on the low branch of a sweet-scented shrub across the creek. Now and then one would dart off into the air, grab a fragile insect, sometimes almost turning a somersault to do so, and then return to the same branch. "I should not mind being a bird," said Mary at last.

Billy had been thinking the same thing.

"I would choose to be the nonpareil," Mary went on. "It is truly the most beautiful, and so prettily colored that it is not readily missed."

"*I* have missed it," Billy told her regretfully. The painted finch, or bunting, did not venture as far north as Pennsylvania, but he had seen its patterned plumage in Mr. Catesby's drawing.

"We shall find thee one before thee returns home," Mary promised.

Billy drew away from his cousin and studied her with a perplexed expression. "Home?" he repeated finally. "Cape Fear is my home now. Thee knows that."

Mary was looking across the glinting water to the flycatchers in their bush. "Thee is like the phoebe, my cousin. Thee will travel far and wide; thee is bound to. But thee will always return to the same branch, and that branch is not here."

Billy did not protest, because, happy though he had been a few moments before, he could not be certain that she was not right. People had always been better judges of him than he was of himself. It was indeed likely, and even desirable, that he travel "far and wide." He might resist returning to Kingsessing, to his "branch," as Mary had called it; he might try with all his strength to stay away; but it was still possible that one day he would go home to the "Hidden River."

For a while they sat silent, throwing out twigs now and then and watching the current carry them away. Billy felt oddly removed, as if already embarked on another journey. This reminded him of something else. "Thy father does not care any more for the savage Indians than does mine," he remarked. "It is an attitude that I find hard to understand."

Mary swung her eyes from the phoebes' shrub to her cousin's face and she stared at him, amazed. "Hard to understand?" she repeated. "Does thee not remember what the Indians did to our grandfather?"

Billy's vague look provided her answer. He admitted that he had no idea of what she was speaking.

"Why, it occurred not far from where we are this moment. At a plantation where they lived. The Indians there killed Grandfather. He had only recently come from the north, after his first wife, thy grandmother, had died. I cannot imagine how thee can have failed to know of it."

Billy sat in a kind of trance, unable to believe what he had heard. The muskrats still scratched in the sand; the dragonflies spread out their lacy wings, the females dipping into the unruffled surface of the creek to deposit their eggs. The pure yellow flowers of the cow lilies reflected the brilliance of the day.

"And my grandmother and father and Aunt Elizabeth were taken away as captives of the Indians and held for ransom. When they were redeemed they went back to Pennsylvania. Father must have truly loved this place to have wished to return here after what had happened."

Billy, who could hardly take it all in, asked when it did happen. The sun shone down on the weathered boards of the bridge, but Billy did not feel warm. He looked at Mary and she seemed to be shivering too.

"It must have been about fifty years ago. Father was a small boy. Just think, Billy, he could have been killed too."

Billy closed his eyes. "Thank God for His mercy in saving him." Still he shook his head. "My father must have known all the circumstances of this atrocity."

Mary said that certainly everyone in the family knew of it, having heard it from the captives themselves.

Yet his father had never mentioned it to his children, Billy was thinking. Was it because he could not bring himself to speak of it, or had he wished to spare them the terror and grief he had known, losing a father in such a way?

As if reading his thoughts, Mary murmured that perhaps she should not have told him. Billy put his arm around her in a reassuring manner. "Oh, but I am thankful that thee did. It explains many things I could not understand and that troubled me. Now I see why my father feels as he does about the barbarous Indians." In a strange way, Billy felt as if a weight had been lifted from him.

"He must be a very brave man to go into the wild country at all, knowing what he does," said Mary.

"And to the Indian councils," Billy added. "Yes, my dear cousin, he is a brave man."

But Mary seemed to be thinking of something else. "Thee knows, Billy, my Aunt Elizabeth died without ever having married. I dread the thought that this might happen to me. Does thee fancy it possible?"

Billy's arm tightened its grasp. "No. I cannot imagine it. In any case, Aunt Elizabeth died young."

"Not young," Mary objected. "She had already passed twenty. Oh, Billy, does thee love me?"

Her cousin laid his lips on her warm forehead, but she raised her head suddenly and kissed his mouth.

By the tree where they had tied their horses, Billy, picking wild strawberries, found a strange flower. "Mary, mark this," he called. "Is it not curious? Has thee ever seen anything like it before?"

Mary crouched beside him and beside the low, fuzzy plant with its reddish two-lobed leaf, but she was not looking at it. "Indeed, my cousin, I have seen nothing like this before," she said softly, her eyes on his intent profile, her hand on his springing hair.

Back at Ashwood, Mary lingered in the coolness of Billy's store, still fragrant with the rough, fresh-cut pine of the floors and walls. "I shall never forget today," she whispered. Her parted lips were rosy with the strawberries Billy had fed her. "Whatever happens to us, I shall never forget it."

As though she had prophesied it, a shadow fell across the open door. Thus it was that Mary's mother found her embracing her cousin.

Mary fled. Billy stood as still as if he would never move again. All he could think of to say was, "Please speak no word of this to my father."

To his astonishment, his aunt smiled at him. "I shall speak no word to thy father, or to thy Uncle William either, who loves thee almost as much. Thee is not to blame, Billy. I know that Mary well. She is spirited and impetuous, and far too forward with young men. She is not like my good Sarah. No, I shall speak no word, but I shall punish Mary later in my own way."

Billy, although not blamed, felt for the first time in his life uncomfortable at Ashwood and sought an excuse to leave it for a while. His opportunity came from a surprising source.

On an April day two years before, Arthur Dobbs, the colonial governor of North Carolina, had written to Peter Collinson about a remarkable plant he had found near the town of Brunswick, inland from Wilmington on the Waccamaw River. A botanist himself, Dobbs had published a book about the flora of the shores of Hudson's Bay and had been in touch from time to time with John Bartram. The plant he described to Collinson he called a "Catch Fly Sensitive which closes upon anything that touches it."

It was small wonder that Collinson was eager to know more about Governor Dobbs's discovery. When he learned that Billy was at Cape Fear, he wrote to John urging him to instruct his son to call upon Dobbs at Brunswick and see the plant, make a drawing, and collect specimens.

There, in the damp pine barrens and open savannas, Billy, following the governor's extended finger, looked down and saw the plant that he and Mary had found among the wild strawberries by the bridge. Carefully he collected specimens to carry back to his father.

There was no doubt in his mind now as to what he must do. He would return to Kingsessing and tell his father of his love for Mary. She was not, after all, his true cousin. Their fathers had been but half brothers, with different mothers. With his father's permission, he would then go back to Ashwood and take Mary away before her own mother might fulfill her mysterious threat of punishment.

Typically, John Bartram was far more impressed with his son's plant specimens than he was with his professions of love, which John dismissed as idle daydreaming. Billy, he felt justified in supposing, was capable of imagining any diversion to lead him away from storekeeping. He named the new flower "Tipitiwitchet," and sent it on to Collinson, along with his son's beautiful drawing, which also included the yellow cow lily, "the round leafed Nymphea as flowering."

Linnaeus, when a dried specimen of "Tipitiwitchet" reached him, called it a miracle of nature and added, "Though I have seen and examined no small number of plants, I must confess I never met with so wonderful a phenomenon."

In the meantime there was no doubt that Billy had been missed at the Precinct of Bladen. "My Dear Brother," William Bartram had written, "the parting with thy son Bille this day felt harder to me than the Parting with my own son, his Behaviour to me & to my family has been so agreeable as well as to others . . ."

William had, in fact, been astonished by Billy's sudden

decision to return to Pennsylvania. He could hardly bring himself to believe it until he actually saw his nephew set out on horseback, with many a sad and backward look.

He had seemed so very happy at Ashwood, particularly recently. William had originally feared that he might miss the company of another cousin, also called Billy, who had gone to Philadelphia to study medicine, as a sort of exchange. But Billy had seemed to enjoy Mary's company just as much; the two were often together. "Bille thinks himself fatter and hartier than ever in his life before," William continued in his letter to his half brother.

Of course the store had not been successful; that was really too much to expect. In explaining what John already knew, William described Billy's disposition as "that of a rover rather than that of a steady worker . . . gentle, modest, contemplative."

In a return letter telling of Billy's safe arrival, his apparent good health, and his happiness in his uncle's plantation, which he had described to his family in the most enthusiastic terms, John spoke of his own longing. "I have a great mind to drink next fall out of the springs at the head of the Cape Fear River," he wrote.

John also wrote of his disappointment in the failure of his son as a trader. "I wish he could gain credit, as Isaac and Moses have," he added, although he realized it was hardly fair to compare Billy with his older brothers. What disturbed him most seemed to be that his son had neglected to send him the seeds he desired from Carolina. He had not received "one single seed from my son who glories so much in the knowledge of plants, and whom I have been at much charge to instruct therein."

Billy was, he could see, in his own restless mind already on his way back to Cape Fear. Sure enough, in the golden blaze of another autumn, Billy Bartram returned to his uncle's house on the Northwest Branch.

He stayed for almost three years. His store continued to lose money; Billy continued to roam in the woods and fields and along the river to his uncle's crystal-clear lake, with its white sand and its millrace fed by underground springs. Sometimes he wandered to wide, saucer-shaped Lake Waccamaw, haunted, it was said, by an Indian maiden. He would imagine that he could see her there, in the rising mists.

Usually he went alone, although occasionally Mary would manage to meet him. Young men were coming to call on her now, from their plantations on the high bluffs—the Robesons from Walnut Grove; the Singletarys, their cousins; and the Browns. Mary would laugh at them, claiming she had no interest in their attentions. As for Billy, if he could not be with Mary, he preferred to be by himself.

He was spending more and more time with his drawings. Peter Collinson had sent him further copies of the pictures of Mark Catesby, the English naturalist who, encouraged by Sir Hans Sloane, had spent much time in Carolina and had published in 1726 his *Natural History of Carolina, Florida, and the Bahama Islands,* the first study of its kind in the New World.

John Bartram sent seeds to Catesby in exchange for the *Natural History,* which John had first seen in 1737 and termed an "excellent performance" when he called upon Thomas Penn in his "best habits," as Collinson had instructed. Catesby had later written to John about a goatsucker he had heard in the south. "There is a bird in Virginia and Carolina, and I suppose in Pennsylvania, that at night calls Whipper Will, and, sometimes, Whip Will's widow, by which name it is called (as the bird clinketh, the fool thinketh). I have neglected to describe it, and therefore should be glad of it. I believe it is a kind of cuckoo."

Collinson had not only advanced money without interest to Catesby so that he might publish his "precious and costly

work on the Flora and Fauna of Carolina in America," but
he had also introduced him to what was rapidly becoming
an international brotherhood, the many young naturalists in
his wide acquaintance. One of these naturalists had been the
Finnish student of Linnaeus, Peter Kalm.

When Kalm had visited the Bartrams at Kingsessing, he
told them about his encounter with the already famous
Catesby. That bird artist had given the inexperienced collector, about to journey to America, detailed advice about
the preserving and shipping of specimens and had also
warned him of the dangers of a strong punch that might be
offered in the colonies—tea and fruit liberally laced with
rum or brandy, he was not sure which.

Kalm had been impressed and enchanted with the quality
of Catesby's drawings, in which, he told the rapt Billy, "he
has incomparably well represented with lifelike colors the
rarest trees, plants, animals, birds, fishes, snakes, frogs, liz-
ards, painted toads . . . so that no one can see that they are
not living where they stand with their natural colors on the
paper." To this high praise Billy had listened intently. It was
even then his desire to be a naturalist and an artist.

Now, more than ten years afterward, Billy was engaged in
making pictures of American birds for George Edwards, the
English ornithologist and another of the innumerable friends
of Peter Collinson. Several years before, Edwards had sent
to Billy, through Collinson, two "curious" books, probably
dealing with avifauna. And in 1758 and again in 1760,
volumes of Edwards's *Gleanings of Natural History* were
published with descriptions of American birds gleaned from
drawings or dried skins received from Billy.

The skins and drawings that Billy sent to George Edwards
and Peter Collinson provided Linnaeus with much of the
information that he needed in his classification of American
birds.

John Bartram wrote to Peter: "He spent his time, this

spring, in shooting and drawing the rare birds of quick passage, which stayed with us but a few days, to rest and fill their bellies, on their flight northward, where they breed, as he observed, by the hens having immature eggs in them, which their quick passage through our country before, rendered them unobserved."

And so it was that more and more often Billy Bartram, in those warm Carolina days, locked the door of his shop and wandered into the beckoning countryside, with his firearm and his sketch block. Unfortunately, errands for his father were also still neglected, even when a friend had come for the very purpose of bearing the packages back to Philadelphia. Billy had not changed. Sadly, John Bartram wrote: "Thee disappointed my expectation much in not sending me any seeds by Captain Sharpless. I know your seeds were some or other ripening from the day thee set foot on Carolina shore to Sharpless' departure, and such as was within a mile or two of thy common walks, or most of them within sight."

On another occasion, the disappointed but always "loving father" chided hopefully: "I don't want to hinder thy own affairs to oblige me; but thee might easily gather a few seeds, when thee need not hinder half an hour's time to gather them, or turn twenty yards out of thy way to pluck them." It all had a very familiar sound.

"Mary, my dearest cousin," murmured Billy, as they sat one day in the empty store, "what can be the matter with me? I know that my father desires seeds, and he is correct that it does not trouble me to find or send them; it is just that I do not think of them. All that seems to be in my mind is drawing, and observing birds and plants, and being with thee."

Mary had brought Billy's lunch to him, as she was in the habit of doing. She began to unpack a stew of squirrel and curlew, and a dish of hominy made by Old Cloe. Billy was not looking at the food. "Mary, thee knows I love thee."

Mary bent further over the hamper and stirred what needed no stirring. Then she looked up with a direct expression. "I love thee too, Billy. I have loved thee since the first time thee ever came here."

She kissed him briefly and rose to her feet. "Did thee ever wonder what might become of me? Whatever thee professes about our not being true cousins, we are cousins just the same. How many nights have I pondered on my pillow what I must say to thee? Can thee believe that I shall always love thee although I marry someone else?"

An image came to Billy's mind of a strong young man with sandy-red hair and the look of a Scot, which he was. "Tom Robeson," he said.

"Tom," Mary echoed, with a faraway look. "Yes, I suppose it was always bound to be Tom. As children we spent much time at Walnut Grove, and they here at Ashwood. Mary Robeson was my first friend. Mary likes thee, Billy."

Billy let this pass.

"I shall say this just once, and never again: I wish it could have been thee. But I spoke to the Friends Meeting at Carvers Creek, and they warned that they would have to read me out. I am marrying out of Meeting, it is true, but I shall not be disowned. I shall have a large family and live at Walnut Grove and be respected. Billy, I kept thinking of Aunt Elizabeth; I could not die a spinster. But I shall doubtless die loving thee as I love thee now. Will thee kiss me once more?"

A gentle smile crossed Billy's face. "I shall kiss thee on thy wedding day," he said.

"Then," Mary murmured slowly, "thee will not be leaving here?"

Billy walked to the window and peered down on the glint-

ing water of Donaho's Creek. "The phoebe," he told her, "is
not yet ready to fly." And, 'My father,' he could not help
thinking, 'will be relieved to hear of this.'

His father, though, had other problems on his mind. England was being ruled by a new king, George III, called
"Farmer George" by some. Collinson wrote that it appeared
the King's father's love of plants may, ironically, have cost
him his life. In 1751 in the Royal Gardens at Kew, Frederick,
the Prince of Wales, had stood in the rain to supervise the
setting-out of some trees. A cold he contracted thereby
brought on a fatal pleurisy.

Might the new king, who was, after all, the grandson and
not the son of George II, possibly grant to John Bartram the
recognition he deserved and appoint him his Royal Botanist,
with a regular stipend? Collinson was hopeful.

John Stuart, a Scotsman and the third Earl of Bute, was a
close friend of the Princess of Wales, and the tutor of her son
George. He was a fierce opponent of Pitt and eventually
succeeded to his high position. He was also a close friend of
Peter Collinson's, and a botanist. Through Collinson he received Bartram's American plants for his garden.

However unpopular he was in the government, there was
no question about the influence he had upon the throne,
even after his fall from power in 1763. Collinson felt confident that his old friend, Lord Bute, could prevail upon
"Farmer George" in Bartram's behalf.

Funds remained vital to John. Much of his family was still
young and needed support. He had patrons in England, it is
true, but, wealthy as they were, they were remarkably slow
in paying. "They are glad of the cargo but apt to forget all
the rest," the harried Collinson apologized.

John Bartram had another reason for desiring funds. For
several years he had cherished a longing to explore the ter-

ritory of Florida, only recently acquired by Britain from Spain. He was in his middle sixties; he might not have strength for many more journeys. "If I could only spend some time in Florida in health," he mused to his friend, Benjamin Franklin, "I believe I could find more curiosities than the English, French, and Spaniards have done in six score of years." And then he had added characteristically, "But the Indians will not let us look at so much as a plant or a tree." To which Ben had replied, "Men can do all things if they will."

It was, in a way, his credo. He had just returned from Britain and was about to sail again. Relations between the colonies and the mother country were deteriorating rapidly. Franklin's greatest concern now was to do all that he could to maintain peace. Just the same, when he left for England that November of 1764, he carried with him a packet of "newly discovered" seeds and roots for the new king.

John waited anxiously to hear how the King had received his present. He had a long wait. When he pressed Collinson for news, Peter reminded him gently that the honor of giving was sufficient.

Still the farmer of Kingsessing waited and grew impatient. "Pray, dear friend," he then begged Ben, "squeese out a few lines as often as Convenience will allow to comfort thy old friend in his new stove room."

And Franklin, who had given Bartram that stove of his own invention, suggested that he sit placidly at home beside it and enjoy his later years. "Digest the knowledge you have acquired, compile and publish the many observations you have made."

It annoyed Franklin, the author, that John Bartram had not written more about his work and discoveries. And now, instead of that, he was chafing to be off again on another adventure. Franklin had no sympathy with journeys for the sake of journeying. "If I could find in any Italian travels," he declared, "a receipt for making Parmesan cheese, it would give me more satisfaction than a transcript of any inscription from any old stone whatever."

Nevertheless, in 1764, wishing that "some notice may be taken of John's merit," he had proposed an allocation of funds for him, that "He might be made happy as well as more useful, by a moderate pension, that would enable him to travel thro' all the New Acquisitions with orders to the Governors and Commanding Officers at the several outposts, to forward & protect him in his Journeys."

Then, in the spring of 1765, the long-awaited letter arrived. "I have the pleasure to inform thee, my good friend," wrote Peter Collinson, "that my repeated solicitations have not been in vain; for this day I received certain intelligence from our gracious King that he hath appointed thee his Botanist, with a salary of fifty pounds a year." Never out of character, Peter could not resist adding: "You don't know the difficulty, trouble and attendance to get things to the King. Though I undertook it for you, I shall not for anybody else."

Word of the appointment spread fast. Most of John's friends were overjoyed by the recognition that had been granted, it was felt, not a day too soon to the farmer of Kingsessing. Surprisingly, Dr. Garden of Charleston raised an objection. He wrote to Linnaeus in Sweden: "Surely John is a worthy man; but yet to give the title of King's Botanist to a man who can scarcely spell, much less make out the characters of any one genus of plants, appears rather hyperbolical."

Alexander Garden's protest was as much political as anything else. In the growing unrest of the colonies, he, as well as many others, remained sympathetic with the mother country, and he understood that John, the supposedly peaceable Quaker, did not. Another mutual friend and a Charleston neighbor, Henry Laurens, presiding at the Provincial Congress of Carolina, was disturbing Garden with his anti-British sentiments, and Garden disapproved of Bartram's association with him.

1765, the year of Bartram's appointment, was also the year of the Stamp Act, the first direct and heavy taxation of the colonists. The act had been passed by Parliament in March, and it was a difficult time for everyone. As in the American Civil War, one hundred years later, brother stood against brother.

By one of those coincidences that helps to make the study of history so fascinating, the first militant resistance to the Stamp Act occurred on the Cape Fear River, where the Philadelphia Quakers living there kept in close touch with Franklin. They understood that he had pleaded their cause eloquently, as only he could, to the House of Commons, insisting that the colonists could be legally charged only with their consent, and that without representation they could never "with the least degree of justice be taxed by Parliament."

"The Stamp Act says we shall have no commerce, make no exchanges of property with each other, neither purchase nor grant nor recover debts; we shall neither marry nor make out wills, unless we pay such and such sums, and this is intended to extort our money from us or ruin us by the consequences of refusing to pay it." So Benjamin Franklin, their representative, explained it to the colonists.

John Dickinson, the lawyer from Philadelphia, was equally irate. "Men cannot be happy," he stated, "without freedom, nor free without security of property. Power," he recognized, "is of a tenacious nature: what it seizes it will retain."

In the midst of all this hubbub, John wrote to Peter Collinson, thanking him for his efforts in his behalf, accepting the high honor of being Royal Botanist, and making plans for his venture into the new and little-known colony of Florida. He was naturally anxious to be among the first to examine this recently acquired territory. It was important that he collect plant specimens and make recommendations for proper land use and cultivation before other, and possibly destructive, explorers arrived.

Yet, in all his eagerness he remained practical. "I am too old to make the trip alone," he had dutifully confessed. And then he added what had been in his mind for a long time: "But I think my son William will be a fit person to accompany me."

Collinson was relieved. He had already cautioned his friend, "As thou grows in years, thou will do well to consider if thy present constitution and habit of body can undergo the fatigue of such an expedition." Now he was quick to praise Billy's ingenuity and suggest that if he were in good health he could be of great service to his father. He did not fail, however, to point out, in an avuncular way, that Billy had "made some mistakes."

John understood all too well that Billy had made mistakes, not the least of which, he considered, was the affection he had allowed himself to feel and express toward his cousin Mary. So far John had made no comment upon the subject; he had felt that by ignoring it he could perhaps diminish it, and perhaps, in any case, he was exaggerating the situation. Mary had, after all, married Tom Robeson two years before and now had a baby boy named Bartram.

Just the same, he had been anxious for some time to have Billy safely removed from the temptations at Cape Fear, whatever they might be. This seemed the perfect opportunity. It was indeed a Godsend. It did not occur to John that his son would hesitate for a moment to accompany the new Botanist to the King into an unexplored and challenging wilderness.

In truth, Billy had been stunned by the news that he had received from his father. He had fully believed that he had been sent to North Carolina for the rest of his life, to keep store and to live, happily or not, in his uncle's home on the Northwest Branch of the river. Now came orders from Kingsessing to close his shop and sell off all his goods at public auction, turning the matter of his debts over to an attorney, who might possibly recover some part of them in an attempt to satisfy his creditors.

The hint that he had been a failure at still another endeavor was thinly veiled. So was the alternative that if Billy did not accompany his father, he would be called back to Pennsylvania to go into business with a merchant whom his sister Ann had married.

Poor Billy, accustomed to turning to his father, now turned to Mary. "What shall I do?" he asked, knowing that all he wanted to hear her say was to stay.

But she did not say it. "Thee has no choice, Billy. Thee must go with thy father." They sat on the dusty steps of the store, while a soft wind swung the Spanish moss on the blackjack oaks. Billy picked up a stick and made some meaningless marks in the sand.

"Thee will enjoy it once thee starts out," Mary said gently. "It will be a new world for thee."

Billy saw in her face that she expected him to go and would be disappointed in him even for demurring. It was true, then, he had no choice.

Still, he protested. "I do not desire a new world. I want no world away from thee. And pray do not say, or think, 'enjoy.' Thee knows I shall enjoy nothing until I am here again."

From the overgrown thicket of an old Cherokee rose, a Carolina wren poured forth its cheerful "turtle, turtle, turtle." It was one of Billy's favorite birdcalls, but he paid no attention to it. "I shan't be long away, my dearest Mary. And thee shall hear from me, whenever there is a chance to send a message. Keep me in thy heart and prayers, as I shall keep thee in mine."

He paused for a moment and looked off into the distance, as though trying to think of something. "That day when we rode into the woods and fields and came to a bridge over the stream—what name had that place?"

Mary looked pleased that he should remember. "I do not know what true name the place has, my Billy. But that stream runs through Colonel James Moore's land, so we always called it Moore's Creek Bridge."

A few weeks later, Billy Bartram left Cape Fear and traveled to Charleston, where he found his father "hearty and in good health and spirits." Together, as they had journeyed before, they headed toward the wilderness, this time into the trackless reaches of the deep south.

CHAPTER 4

WILDERNESS
YEARS

"Oh, Botany, delightfulest of all sciences!"

Peter Collinson

Billy Bartram finished the pomegranate he had been eating
and leaned back against the trunk of a tupelo tree. The day's
ride had been the most difficult yet, through low swampy
land tangled with high grass and briars. The summer just
past was the hottest and rainiest that most of the Georgia
settlers could remember. Even though it was now October 1,
and the sun shone brightly through the coloring foliage,
broad sheets of water still stood in the flat places. Bridges
had been flooded out, and Billy and his father had had to
force their horses to swim over some of the creeks.

That day they had journeyed twenty miles on their steady
way south from Charleston. The original plan had been to
arrive in St. Augustine, the capital of Florida, early in October. That had meant traveling more than five hundred
miles in a month. From the beginning, Billy had half hoped
that his father would become discouraged by the rigors of
the trip and decide to turn back.

In South Carolina they had both been badly bitten by

mosquitoes. Typically, John, in his enthusiasm, had wandered in the Charleston gardens under a high sun he was not accustomed to. Like Franklin before him, Peter Collinson, on hearing it, had shaken his head and chided his foolish friend. "To think a wise man should have so little prudence!" he had written.

Both Dr. Garden and Henry Laurens had urged John to reconsider this wilderness trek. They worried about his being sixty-six, about Billy's never having been robust, and about both of them being innocent and inexperienced concerning the hazards of the land where they were going.

But it seemed that the more they persuaded, the more determined John was to continue. George III desired a detailed report of the territory received from Spain, a report of its practical aspects as well as of the land itself, with its flora and fauna, its forests and waterways, and particularly its possibilities. What could be accomplished in a profitable way was on the minds of the King's ministers. How could they best make use of their new acquisition? Bartram, as Royal Botanist, was the one to make these determinations.

Furthermore, his physical condition was never better, he declared. His stamina had always been remarkable. With a mission such as this before him, he seemed, if anything, to garner additional strength. His enthusiasm remained unflagging. Sadly, Billy wrote to Mary that it appeared there was little hope of an early return to Cape Fear.

Now he looked out at the Georgia landscape with a bleakness the scene did not reflect. The sun, lower but still brilliant, sent sparks of light from the glossy leaves of the great magnolias, still wet from drenching rains and daily thunderstorms. Ground robins scratched in the damp debris of the forest floor, and now and then one would spring into a scrub oak and call a whistled "jor-ee." A young deer slipped like a shadow through the palmettos.

Earlier that morning Billy had glimpsed a flock of wild

turkeys. Where they foraged for acorns under the live oaks, they appeared so much the color of their background that, when motionless, they were almost impossible to detect. Billy had often marveled at the natural camouflage of animals. Just the same, he would like to have stopped and shot a fine hen for dinner.

His father, though, had protested that they had no time for the hunting or the roasting of a bird. Bread and fruit seemed to satisfy him on his journey; sometimes they found nuts and berries. The autumn woods offered adequate sustenance.

Still, Billy thought wistfully of the venison stew and broth, the sausage meat made from wild hog, and the pilloes of his uncle's table. Pilloe was the local name for pilau, or pilaf, a Persian and Turkish dish of meat, usually lamb or chicken cooked in oil with rice, sometimes with eggplant and tomatoes, and always with spices. At Ashwood, pilloes, or purlews as they were also called, came to the table as large platters of rice baked with shrimp, plover, pineywoods squirrel, or whatever kind of game was on hand. Billy tried not to dwell upon them.

Through the tree trunks he glimpsed what looked like a river. He had not noticed it before. Glancing at his father, who was busily writing in his journal and did not look up, Billy took his gun and headed toward the water in search of ducks.

Along the sandy shore of what now appeared to be a fairly wide river, bald cypresses rose, dripping moss, in which migrating warblers were hunting for insects. Billy had to agree with his father that the cypress stood "in the first order of North American trees," with "its majestic stature, the stateliness of its trunk lifting its cumbrous top toward the skies and casting a wide shade upon the ground, as a dark intervening cloud."

On this late afternoon, a flock of emerald and topaz

parakeets, the "Parakeeto's," of William Hilton, were fluttering about the branches, looking to see if the seeds, their favorite food, had ripened. A huge woodpecker, larger than a crow, with a cream-colored beak and prominent white patches on its wings, was hammering on another cypress nearby, around whose knees green herons and snowy egrets were probing their long bills into the shallows.

Billy stood at the water's edge. At that point the river seemed to bend to the southeast in much the same way that the Northwest Branch had done where it flowed past Ashwood. 'If I looked behind me,' dreamed Billy, 'I could see the house.' But of course there was no house, nor any for miles around, only the uninhabited land stretching out on every side toward the wet woods and the distant glowing hills, and only the warblers and parakeets and the woodpecker to make a sound.

Years later, Billy was to praise the great river with its "scenes of primitive, as yet unmodified by the hand of man." Now all he saw was emptiness.

There were no ducks on the water. Billy turned and made his way slowly back to his father.

That gentleman was not sitting upon the ground writing in his journal as Billy had left him. He came, instead, breaking through the underbrush in a state of some excitement. "Billy, where has thee been? I have been awaiting thee. A most curious shrub, or small tree, I cannot say which, is growing nearby, one which we have not found before. It resembles somewhat the loblolly bay, and yet it is not like it. I am satisfied that this is a new species, but come and give me thy opinion."

It was typical of John's understanding and gentleness that he consult his son, whose opinion, they both knew, might not be of great value.

The "curious" shrub, or small tree, about twenty feet tall, was growing not far from the riverbank among bays, low oaks and palmettos, and the ever-present, stately long-leafed pines. It had slender, pointed, alternate, and glossy springing leaves, upraised in clusters like open chalices. In the sunset light they held a rosy glow. Billy, on looking closer, observed that they were indeed beginning to turn rosy themselves, assuming an autumn coloration that many of the trees around them already bore.

The flowers had blossomed and fallen, but obviously not long ago, since the brown petals were readily apparent strewn under the striped gray trunk. Seeds, not yet mature even on this first day of October, gave further indication of the plant's late blooming.

"Billy, I am convinced that this is an entirely new tree and not the other that we have been finding in the Georgia swamplands and their borders. It is a great loss to us that the seeds are not yet ripe for gathering."

Billy took his small sketch pad from his pocket and made a rough drawing of the tree and its leaves, its beginning seed pods and its fallen petals. He thought, 'Someday I shall come here again and draw the flowers. And I'll come once in the late fall and gather the ripe seeds.'

"Well, Billy," his father was saying briskly. "Does thee imagine that time is a river upon which we can float forever? Governor Grant is at this very moment expecting us in St. Augustine. Mr. Laurens was kind enough to make the appointment, and we are already days behind our schedule."

Henry Laurens, born in Charleston in 1724, had traveled to London to become a clerk in a countinghouse, and then returned to Charleston to set up a countinghouse of his own and engage in trade with the colonies, particularly in the field of planting. He had met Governor Grant in 1761 in South Carolina when Grant had led the final expedition against the Cherokees. Later he became Grant's private business agent. So it was only natural that, when he learned that his friend John Bartram was planning an exploratory mission in Florida for the King, he insisted upon his meeting with a man who could surely help him more than any other—the new governor.

Grant had already urged Laurens to aid him in planning the development of his province. Laurens felt that few could be more qualified in this respect than the farmer of Kingsessing, who had become the friend of Franklin and Washington as well as of the foremost statesmen and naturalists on both sides of the ocean.

So Laurens had arranged a meeting between the two, and Grant, who had already planned a congress with the Lower Creek Indians that autumn to decide upon a boundary line, suggested to Bartram that he might find it worthwhile to be present.

Billy had watched anxiously as his father considered this. He had not, after thinking it over for some time, divulged to his family that he knew of the fate of his Grandfather William, he simply stayed very quiet when his father railed against the barbarous savages.

Henry Laurens had persuaded John to go to the congress. Now, on their way there, Billy indulged in his favorite pastime—composing a letter in his mind. "My dearest cousin," he began. "Thee will doubtless be astonished to read where we are passing the next few days. The place is called Picolata, on the banks of the river of San Juan, and we are here with Governor James Grant, of East Florida, to meet with the Creek Indians and arrange for a peace concerning the fixing of a boundary."

At the place called Picolata, or "Pass of the Salamatoto River," the stream narrowed, forming a natural crossing for Indians, and later for the Spaniards making their way westward. A Spanish fort had been built there in 1700 to protect the crossing and the trail, known as the "old Spanish highway," which by then reached northwest to the Gulf of Mexico.

Not far from the fort, on this warm November morning, a pavillion of fresh green pine branches had been constructed to shade the governor and his party. Colorful flags stood here and there in the clearing. From the distance came the sound of drumming, and down the sandy road that ran along the river's edge marched a company of drummers and fifers, and behind them officers of the Royal Artillery from the garrison in St. Augustine, resplendent in their dress uniforms. The sun in a cloudless sky glittered on polished silver and brass, the silk of banners, and the metallic glints of braid.

Most of the Indians had already arrived and were encamped along the riverbank. They were also a colorful band. To Billy the whole scene had a fantastic and unrealistic quality. There in that rustic wilderness setting, the gaudily costumed groups, waiting to begin the congress, seemed somewhat like actors about to assume their parts in an outdoor masque or pageant.

The reason for the delay was that the expected barge from the capital, bearing an array of presents for the Indians, had not yet arrived. Billy, after inquiring of his father as to the condition of his health, took advantage of the lull to wander into the palmetto-lined swamps.

Although John had said little about it, Billy realized that his father was not at all well. A fever, and perhaps jaundice, that had come upon him in Charleston, possibly as a result of his incautious noontime exploring, had left him weak and exhausted. He slept more than was his wont, and sudden movements seemed an effort for him. Still, he had insisted that as an acknowledged representative of the King he must attend the congress. Billy, by now accustomed to his company, felt oddly alone as he sat on a fallen cypress log by a sandy spit of land and surveyed the river.

His San Juan, now anglicized to St. Johns, was originally called the Welaka by the Indians who raked its oysters and built up their shell mounds along its banks. In 1562, the French explorer Jean Ribault christened it Rivière de Mai because he had first seen it in that month. There is still a town at its mouth called Mayport.

Conquistadors, dismayed by the speed of the current's flow where it met the ocean's breakers, renamed it Rio de Corrientes. When Pedro Menéndez founded St. Augustine and the Mission of San Mateo there, he also changed the name of the river to San Mateo, for Saint Matthew. When the mission became San Juan's, so did the great stream running past the capital.

Like the Nile, it is one of the few rivers this side of the equator that flows north from its source. Looking at it from his seat on the fallen cypress, Billy wondered how this would affect the water journey his father was planning to undertake in an effort to discover the original spring from which the great flow stemmed.

It sometimes seemed to Billy that his whole life had been composed of rivers, or segments of them. There had been the last one, where they had studied the curious tree, and the first one, upon whose shores he had been born.

And then there had been the Cape Fear River. He had received only one letter from Mary in return for the many he had written. And she had said very little. She had mentioned the growing and active resentment of the Quaker community at Carvers Creek against England as a result of the Stamp Act. Mr. Franklin was working hard for peace, but in his letters he was not reassuring. Many Cape Fear families were eager for open rebellion. She mentioned her joy in her son, Bartram Robeson, now more than a year old, and her longing for another child. Tom was often away; her days were lonely. Billy's pensive face grew wistful.

Then he heard his father calling and turned quickly to go.

Yet, as Billy nearly reached him, John called out again, crying, "Stop! Stop! Stop still where thee stands! Mark the path before thee."

Billy looked down and saw a huge rattlesnake coiled in the path, not three feet away. Billy had seen these reptiles before, in the Catskill Mountains and in Connecticut, but he had never watched one set and prepared to strike at him. He had no choice, he recounted afterwards with an ingenuous apology for his lack of mercy, but to kill "the monster." He dispatched the snake with a hastily cut sapling and dragged the six-foot length of diamond-link scales back to the clearing, where he suddenly found himself the center of an "amazed multitude, both Indians and my countrymen."

He had no doubt that his father had saved his life. Another step forward would have doubtless been his last. Just a moment before, he had been thinking resentfully of Tom Robeson. Now all he felt in his heart was thankfulness.

And he was about to have another surprise. James Grant, professing to be fond of rattlesnake meat, sent word to Billy to deliver the serpent to his cooks. An invitation was sent to the Bartrams to dine at the governor's table that very evening, when the rattlesnake was "served up in several dishes." John, always eager to taste new and unusual food, particularly that which came from the wilderness, pronounced it delicious and wondered whether His Majesty might have any interest in its economic value as a comestible. Billy, remembering his narrow escape and also his regret at having to kill the snake, tasted but could not swallow the meat.

Running against the current, the barge from St. Augustine finally appeared around the river bend, with its presents for the Indians: silver medals and chains, blankets and tobacco, a little rum. Guns from the Spanish fort signaled the ship's arrival, and that was all that the Indians needed to begin their shouting and dancing to the accompaniment of rhythms shaken from their rattle boxes. Their gleaming skin was patterned in paint; their multicolored feathers bobbed; they bore down upon the governor like a gaudy flock of tropical birds.

Billy watched with a fascination not unmixed with anxiety. Yet all that the noisy troop did was stroke the white men's heads with the eagle feathers dangling from their peace pipes.

Governor Grant took a calumet and smoked it, and for two full days the congress continued. Billy, sitting rigidly beside his father, longed for it to be over. On all sides, beyond the pavillion, he heard bird songs that he could not recognize. On all sides, in the swamps and pine barrens and on the grassy savannas, must be growing plants that no man had ever described. And before him, just beyond the palmettos, ran the great river whose source had not yet been found. He chafed at the ceremonial speechmaking that went on and on.

He had no choice, though, but to wait patiently. His father slept or rested on the ground, and he counted on Billy to take his notes for him. So Billy put down in his book as much as he could understand, and sketched the Indians in their plumage, and rejoiced when the negotiations drew to a close.

So, apparently, did all assembled. Grant, pleased with the advantageous treaty he had made, passed out silver medals and other presents, and signed the paper on behalf of George III for "Perfect, Sincere, and perpetual Peace." Actually, he would have liked to have maneuvered for even more land for the King, but, as he told John Bartram later, he decided to wait a while and "let our Creek Friends breathe a little."

The Creeks, who in their excitement had given up more land than they intended, seemed delighted with their gifts. The chiefs signed the paper with their various marks; both races pledged to live in friendship side by side; and a festive banquet was laid out with more than a little rum passed from hand to hand.

It was now time to start upon the long-awaited expedition up the San Juan to its source, a trip which no white man had ever made, or recorded if he had. Father and son had possibly lingered too long already, enjoying the governor's hospitality in St. Augustine and waiting for John to recover. Both Bartrams were surprised by the December chill in the Florida air and by the hoarfrost on the ground.

Governor Grant had been particularly interested in this journey to search for the head of the river. He presented John with a private subsidy of twenty-five pounds; but, much more than that, he provided a dugout canoe called a "battoe," a guide-and-deer-hunter, and a cook-and-rower.

It was not only the expedition that concerned him. Grant was also anxious for a firsthand report of a couple of trading posts along the river. By 1765 there were only five stores that were licensed to trade with the Indians. There the Creeks brought skins and venison and shopped for clothing and paint. A man named James Spalding, from St. Simons Island in Georgia, had set up two of these trading posts. They were known simply as the Upper and Lower Stores. The Upper Store was located at the southern end of a large lake in the river; the Lower Store was at the north end of this lake, diplomatically named George. Two days after Christmas, the Bartram party arrived at the Lower Store.

They had had a windy voyage. Much of the time the choppy water had forced them to land and make their way along the riverbank, often venturing deep into the sheltering woods, where, on Christmas Eve, the hunter had killed a deer and the cook a turkey.

Christmas Day they feasted. On a high point of land,

which because of the quantity of Seville oranges growing
there John imagined had once been part of a Spanish plantation, the explorers ate their dinner of turkey and venison.
Above them live oaks with trunks two feet in diameter
spread their gnarled branches. Behind them towered magnolias and hickories. In the swamps below grew loblolly
bays and maples. A hollow pine with bees swinging around
it oozed with sweet honey. John made a kind of dessert by
cutting off one end of a sour orange and pouring the wild
honey in, as he had seen the Indians do.

Always he offered a silent grace. On this holiday, even
though far away from his family and garden, and still not
entirely recovered from his debilitating fever, he felt a sense
of contentment. The sun blazed into the clearing; cardinals,
wrens, and ground robins called on all sides. He was where
he had wanted so long to be. His dearest son, Billy, was with
him.

He remembered a letter he had written to his son several
years before. It was as true now as then. "My guardian angel
seemed to direct my steps," he had said. "The presence of
God was with me, and my heart overflowed with praises and
humble adoration to him, both day and night, in my wakeful
eyes." Aloud he offered a second thanks to this Creator.

Billy had bowed his head as much in respect for his father
as in gratitude to God. It was true that he had eaten his
Christmas dinner with zest and had savored the smoky,
freshly roasted meat and the wilderness scene around him,
but in truth he would have preferred cold squirrel and
hominy brought by Mary to the confines of his Cape Fear
store. With luck, in a day or two they would arrive at Mr.
Spalding's Lower Trading Post. And there would surely be a
letter from his cousin waiting for him.

"Mark, Billy," his father was saying, pointing a stocky
finger, "a nonpareil." And Billy looked up in time to see the
beautifully colored painted finch, or bunting, flash like a

jeweled butterfly through the low bushes. It was the first one that he had ever seen, though he had searched and searched. It was the bird that Mary had said she would like to be. For a moment he felt transported to that June day and the bridge over Moore's Creek. He sensed his father's eyes on him in a curiously tender way. "The nonpareil was a fine Christmas present, Father," he said.

On January 26, exactly one month from the day when they had first arrived at the trading post, they were back again at the Lower Store. They had traveled the length of Lake George to the Upper Store and from there on up the river. They had seen many wonderful sights, some never before looked upon by white men. There had been groves of wild cherry and orange trees, "either full of fruit or scattered on the ground, where the sun can hardly shine for the green leaves," as John recorded in his journal.

They had seen dark virgin cypress stands and a huge spring that churned up from a clear lake bottom five fathoms below, with multitudes of fish in the transparent depths and alligators swimming or lying like logs upon the shore. Both Billy and his father had been impressed and fascinated with the spring. "What a surprising fountain it must be," John wrote, "to furnish such a stream, and what a great space of ground must be taken up in the pinelands, ponds, and savannahs and swamps to support and maintain so constant a fountain, continually boiling right up from under the deep rocks."

They had heard wolves howling and discovered a wood rat, describing it for science for the first time. Then, finally, on January 12, they had come to a sandy shoal in the river, where "the weeds and reeds stopped our battoe in such a manner that it was impossible to push her any farther."

Thus they had arrived at the farthest navigable point on

their journey up the San Juan. The actual source, they supposed, lay in the extensive draining marshes "which opened toward the southeast, how far beyond our view we could not determine. The water reeds grew here in the current as thick and close together as on the marsh, that is, as close as hemp; yet the current forceth its way through, and also under the great patches of the . . . other water plants, which are all entangled together, covering many thousands of acres."

Billy sprang from the battoe and stood in the water, so that he would be able to say he had landed at the head of navigation. His father sat and stared at the saw grass, and it was difficult to say whether he was sad or relieved that they could venture no farther.

As for himself, Billy was disappointed that the source of such a wide and splendid river should not be a great spring gushing forth from a crystalline pool, such as they had seen along the way. It would be far more fitting to the magnitude of the stream than this vague and inconsequential trickling from the reedy shallows.

The boat was poled from the sand and pointed in the opposite direction. And that night, for the first time on the voyage, the explorers slept in the same clearing where they had made camp the evening before.

On the return journey they chose as many different routes as possible, taking new branches and crossing unfamiliar lakes. Now and then they ventured along the west, or "Indian," side. On the second morning the hunter shot a male bear, which he estimated must weigh four hundred pounds. Neither Billy nor his father had ever tasted bear meat before, and they found rather to their surprise that it was "very mild and sweet. It was not hunger that engaged us in its favor," John recorded, "for we had a fat young buck and three turkeys fresh shot at the same time."

They delayed a day so that the cook could barbecue the

bear and thus preserve it for their meals on their way back down the river. They cut the hearts from the cabbage palms and stewed them in bear oil. John, who obviously appreciated good food, did not fail to note in his journal: "I never eat half as much cabbage at a time, and it agreed the best with me of any sauce I ever ate, either alone or with meat." He went on to praise the site of the feast in the most complimentary way possible: "This situation pleased me so much we called it Bartram's Bluff."

Sometimes vast floating islands of sea lettuce "growing all in a mat" impeded their way. Billy was amazed to see these drifting rafts, upon which gallinules and egrets picked their way about as if on land. Later he was to describe them as "delightful green plains," creating "a most picturesque appearance . . . completely inhabited and alive with crocodiles, serpents, frogs, otters, crows, herons, curlews, jackdaws, etc."

Now, however, any deterrent to their progress disturbed him. Not only was he eager to reach Spalding's Upper Store to look for a letter from Mary but he was also concerned about his father. In spite of his excellent appetite, he had seemed to become indolent as the days grew warmer; gnats and mosquitoes bothered him greatly; the sun made him slightly feverish; and the glare from the water hurt his eyes. None of this would John Bartram divulge by manner or complaint, but his watchful son read the signs. He was relieved then when at the Upper Store Trading Post the wind blew so hard that they could not venture onto the lake the next morning, and his father could rest.

There had been no letter from Mary. Billy, always seeking for explanations, concluded that the carrier had fallen into the hands of hostile Indians, or perhaps stepped into a quicksand or sinkhole, or been attacked by alligators. Eager for distraction, he joined the keeper of the store and some other men at a pineland pond, where they spent the afternoon shooting the wild geese that dropped down to feed on the fresh grasses growing there.

On January 24, Billy discovered a new plant. "A lovely sweet tree," his father called it, "with leaves . . . which smelled like sassafras and produced a very strange kind of seed pod . . . a charming bright evergreen, aromatic." This shrub turned out to be the licorice-perfumed anise.

Two days later they arrived at the Lower Store.

The letter from Mary was as mystifying as the sight of it had been welcome. Where Billy had openly poured out his heart to his cousin, she in return had had little to say. She had been grateful for his communications, which, it appeared, she had shared with her husband since she added that he also enjoyed the accounts of the journey. Then she had ended with what seemed a very strange remark. She hoped, she said, that he would stop at Cape Fear to visit them on his way home to Philadelphia.

Billy walked out onto the porch of the store. Deer hides were tacked on the rough boards, and a rattlesnake skin was stretched above the door. Hams from wild hogs hung here and there, along with some drying corn. Billy looked past them to where the lake created by a widening of the river spread out, a pale, misty blue. Palms along the edges raised their pompous heads. In the blurred flatness they seemed to tower. And over all, the sun filtered down through high, fine clouds, and a sudden gust of wind swirled the surface of the water.

Within him, Billy felt the stirring of an idea. Men came and went, stamping with their boots on the floor, kicking off the inevitable, ubiquitous sand, but Billy paid them no heed. The idea grew and developed until it seemed to be less an idea than a reality, and then the only possible answer.

Until now he had not thought much about the future. He had merely assumed that he would return to North Carolina and resume his life where he had so abruptly left it off. The suggestion of going back to Kingsessing had simply not occurred to him.

By that evening his decision had become irrevocable. "Father," he said with evident sadness, "I shall not be going home with thee."

To John, who had only just begun to feel robust again after his fevers and other sufferings, this must have been a very harsh blow. No doubt he heard the words with well-justified incredulity. "What then," he asked after a moment, "what then does thee intend to do?" Was it possible that his son was thinking of returning to Ashwood, where all had gone so disastrously?

One incredible statement followed another. "I intend to remain here in East Florida."

"Here?" To his bewildered father, "here" was James Spalding's Lower Store. He was a practical man, and in his shocked state his thoughts ran to immediacies.

"Here in East Florida," repeated Billy, with a faraway look. "I think near that place where the congress was held. The land by the river there was pretty for growing things, and it is but a short journey to the capital, should I want for supplies."

John Bartram stood shaking his head. To him Picolata had been anything but pretty; to him it had been the most desolate of all the new country. It was true, of course, that his illness, coupled with his enduring fear of Indians, might have heightened his distaste for the place. "What," he asked at last, "does thee plan to grow?"

Billy had deliberated everything. "Why, indigo, Father. Mr. Laurens reported that it was an export crop welcomed in Britain for the dying of fabric and garments, and that the indigo grown in East Florida was of the highest quality. Prices, he said, range from three to eight shillings for the pound," he added hopefully.

Henry Laurens would be in a position to know. As an agent, as well as a planter himself, he acted in behalf of other growers, supplying them with rice, rum, and slaves, and helping them market their crops. He was an advisor of many British investors with land interests in the newly acquired territory.

As a resident of Charleston, Laurens was in an advantageous situation. St. Augustine, on the river, was guarded from the sea by a sandbar which made ocean-going shipments impossible. Goods, therefore, went overland from the capital to Charleston, and thence to Britain. British products arrived in East Florida by the same route. The astute Laurens was able to watch what came and went. He had quickly assessed the importance of indigo.

There was little that John Bartram could say in opposition to such pleading. He told Billy that he would do all he could to help him finance his dream of an indigo plantation. He then arranged and paid for six slaves to clear the land and aid in the setting-out and the harvesting. A farmer from a totally dissimilar part of the world, he had only the barest notion of what was involved for Billy in the south. He begged him not to overlook planting a few crops for his own sustenance, and then, still bewildered, he made the long voyage back to Kingsessing alone. It was not until June that he could bring himself to tell his friend Peter Collinson what had befallen.

He wrote painfully: "I have left my son Billy in Fla. Nothing will do with him now, but he will be a planter upon St. John's River, about twenty-four miles from Augustine, and six from the Fort of Picolata. This frolic of his, and our maintenance, hath drove me to great straits."

John, his health restored, was engaged in the preparation of his report for the King. Rumors had reached England that the long peninsula was little more than an unlikely combination of sandy desert and mosquito-haunted swamp, with no economic value at all. John, with a heavy heart, found himself with the ironic duty of pointing out the advantages of settling there.

But Billy's "whim," as his father now called it, had cost him more than heartache. Tactfully he tried to indicate to Collinson that his fifty-pound stipend ought to be increased.

Collinson replied that he had done all that he could. "Thou knows the length of a chain of fifty links," he wrote. "Go as far as that goes, and when that's at an end, cease to go farther."

He continued, however, to be impressed by Billy's "fine drawings" and his "pretty way of drying fish." He requested some southern seeds for the patrons who were weary of the old ones, and he suggested that Billy include in his shipments some butterflies, which, "in such a climate are certain to increase in size and beauty, with many new species to be found only there."

To Billy he also sent an encouraging word, saying that he was "glad to see thee has not lost that curious art which so few attain. I wish it could any way be turned to thy profit." And the kind man added, "I can truly say I have never had thee long from my mind, and watched for any opening that might prove advantageous."

By midsummer, John's report, *An Account of East Florida, with a Journal by John Bartram of Philadelphia,* was completed and ready to be sent to the King via Peter Collinson. With it went maps, surveys, and drafts of the San Juan and of its various lakes and tributaries. Soil samples, fossils, shells, and a collection of dried plants and bird skins were also included. Most important to John was a set of Billy's drawings which he sent along in the parcel.

The Royal Botanist presented a generally realistic picture of the country he had explored, shading it slightly on the optimistic side. He suggested that the marshlands could be drained dry for the planting of corn and indigo, and partially drained for growing rice. He praised the great domes of cypress that could be cut for lumber and shingles, the live oaks for shipbuilding, the straight long-needled pines for spar masts and yardarms, for turpentine and pitch. He wrote of grove after grove of oranges, of the rivers teeming with bass and bream and trout, and of the sea abounding with shellfish. He described fountains and springs "big enough to turn a mill."

Besides his recommendations, it was natural for John to include his observations of flora and fauna, plantations and entertainments, and even a history of recorded hurricanes.

In the meantime, a Dr. William Stork, botanist and member of the Royal Society, had come to the southern territory as an agent involved in land grants. His highly favorable opinion of the new acquisition, an *Account of East Florida,* was published before John's.

In the next year, 1767, Dr. Stork's *Account* was reissued in London, and with it, in the same volume, John Bartram's *Journal.* Two years later, still another edition was published.

Henry Laurens sat on the porch of Governor Grant's country place, a plantation of six thousand acres called "The Villa." Before him lay field after field of indigo, tended by forty slaves who drooped now in the heat of the August afternoon. Laurens had just come from the capital and he was warm and thirsty. An oleander by the corner of the porch offered some shade, but there was no breeze from the meadows. A servant came with a silver beaker of punch made from sugar and rum and sour oranges, and with the information that His Excellency had been detained in town and would arrive presently.

Compared with Charleston, St. Augustine was indeed only a town, but it was rapidly growing. At least two ships a month arrived from South Carolina, bringing elegant English furniture and reluctant African slaves, and taking away indigo, turpentine, and hides. The governor gave balls, with guests in powdered wigs and jewels. Citizens of a number of countries came and went, surprised at the sophistication of the town, the salubrious air, the omnipresent flowers, and the brightly uniformed regiments marching with their banners past the handsome old Spanish fort of San Marcos.

This was the scene Henry Laurens tried to think about as he sat in what little coolness The Villa's porch provided and awaited the arrival of his host. But there was another, more vivid, picture in his mind, and the thought of the capital made that one all the more depressing. He had been, that week, to call on Billy Bartram.

One could hardly consider it "calling." He had traveled thirty miles over a road full of stumps and washouts and so sunken that in wet weather it would most certainly be impassable. On a particularly low "sheet of sandy pine barren, verging on the swamp," he had found Billy near a marshy inlet of the St. Johns.

The situation was, he allowed to Governor Grant, who had now arrived and received his cup of punch, "the least agreeable of all the places that I have seen. The river there was almost stagnated, which must make the whole plantation unhealthy, as well troublesome to come at by water, especially in dry seasons."

"The hovel that he lives in is extremely confined and hardly proof against the weather. And, sir, by its very location it is bound to be hot, in fact the only disagreeably hot place that I have found in East Florida. You must be aware that I am not normally affected by extremes of temperature, and yet today . . ." He sighed, and took from his pocket a large silk handkerchief with which he began to fan himself.

"And, Billy," asked Grant, guiding the conversation back, "how does he fare?"

Henry Laurens flapped his handkerchief once more and let it fall into his lap. "That is what has depressed me the most. You are aware that he appears delicate; now he is looking more frail and delicate than ever. I am very much afraid that he is in imperfect health, perhaps even suffering from fever. No indigo is growing for him. He plants it in the sand, and the rain or flood tides wash it away. The six slaves his father gave him are of no help whatsoever. Of them, only two know how to handle an axe tolerably and one of these threatened Billy's life, for what reason I do not know. It is difficult to think of Billy inflaming anyone."

"And what provisions has he to sustain him?" asked the governor, looking worried.

"Very little that I could see," Laurens replied. "A patch of rice, a few yams and beans, hardly enough for seven men; though in truth one be barely a child in arms. His provision of grain, flesh, and spirits is scant even to penury. Naturally I left what little I could carry to him. Because, worst of all, there is no friend, or neighbor, indeed no human inhabitant within nine miles by water, and there is no boat."

The governor of the new territory, who obviously had many problems to ponder, seemed to have put everything else out of his mind. "We shall have to do something at once," he declared. "We must inform his father."

"I have already taken the liberty to write to John Bartram," Laurens said gravely. "I penned the letter in my mind on my way back from Billy, and this afternoon, while awaiting your return, I put my thoughts to paper. I implored Mr.

Bartram to rescue his son, whose pride, obviously, would not allow him to make such a plea himself. I laid stress upon the forlorn state of this worthy and ingenious lad, who could prosper in a suitable environment but cannot prosper here. He is a passing fine artist; I have seen his work. But he has had discouragements enough to break the spirits of any man, and has been exposed to more difficulties than those whose crimes drive them to exile. All of this I wrote to Mr. Bartram."

James Grant sat silent for a moment. Then he said, "You did well, Henry. His father would want to know that; he has even gone so far as to ask me to find it out, as I told you. But let us hope that Billy, with his artless pride, never discovers what you have written."

It was Henry Laurens's turn to sit silent. He set down his punch cup on the silver tray and looked out across the acres of fertile indigo, upon which the sun was casting its last rays. "Indeed, Your Excellency," he said at last, "it was Billy who begged me to write it."

The next fall found Billy back at Kingsessing. He took a job as a day laborer on a nearby farm, as he had done before, and it seemed to him as though his life had swung around in a kind of circle, with all that time in between and nothing accomplished. He was twenty-eight years old, he told himself, and what had he done with his life? His youth was over; one failure had followed another, and here he was back home again, haying on the Schuylkill. He spent his days working as hard as his strength and energy would allow, and he tried not to think too much about the diaster at Picolata, which had been far more crushing to him than any of his other failures.

His family and friends were also deeply concerned by

what Peter Collinson had termed "William's unsteady con-duct." It was indicative of Collinson's concern that he called him "William" instead of "Billy."

"Nothing but marrying will settle him," he wrote to John. "With a prudent, discreet woman, he may return to Florida, and amend his conduct." Typically, in the eagerness of his conviction, he had gone on to describe this woman as "such as knows how to share the toils as well as the comforts of a married state. If this is not done," he had added direfully, "he'll fall into the snares of a loose, unlawful way of life, from whence no good can come, but much evil and incon-venience."

In July of 1768, Peter Collinson wrote still another letter. In it he recounted that Lady William Henry Cavendish Bentinck, the Duchess of Portland, had dined with him. This in itself would hardly have been remarkable. The reason for the letter was to inform John and Billy that he had shown Her Highness a parcel of Billy's drawings which had arrived that very morning, and that the duchess had been delighted.

"So great was the deception, it being candlelight," Collin-son described the scene, that they had disputed for some time whether the pictures were engravings or drawings. The duchess's delight was such that she forwarded twenty guineas to Billy with an order for "all Land, River and your sea Shells, from the very least to the greatest . . . not be crowded and most carefully done."

Finally, Peter Collinson found yet another patron for Billy, a man who would influence, aid, and ultimately alter and conserve the river of his life. "This morning," Peter wrote to John Bartram, "Dr. Fothergill came and break-fasted here. As I am thoughtful how to make Billy's in-genuity turn to some advantage, I bethought of showing the Doctor his last elegant performance. He deservedly admired them . . ."

John Fothergill was born in Yorkshire in 1712 of a Quaker

family. After studying medicine at the College of Physicians in Edinburgh, he moved to London to practice, specializing in ailments of the throat. Among his patients were Lord Grenville, the Prime Minister, Lord Clive, and John Wesley. Fothergill also attended Benjamin Franklin during the years when Franklin lived in London.

It was natural that such a man should be acquainted with Peter Collinson. Actually, they were more than acquaintances; they had become intimate friends. It was Collinson who had inspired Fothergill to plant an extensive and selective garden at his home in Upton, Essex, which the wool merchant later described as a "paradise of plants." In fact, the doctor, writing to Linnaeus, declared that no one who shared Peter's comradeship could "do other than cultivate plants."

Fothergill had also been writing to John Bartram ever since Collinson had introduced them by correspondence around the middle of the century. John and others had sent him such flourishing seeds that the president of the Royal Society had asserted that Fothergill's "paradise" was "equalled only by Kew," and that "no other garden in Europe had so many scarce and valuable specimens."

At breakfast that morning in July 1768, Dr. John Fothergill not only admired Billy's work but he also commissioned him to draw a series of shells and turtles, particularly those seen in Florida, together with their complete descriptions, and at his own price. "Set all thy wits and ingenuity to work to gratify such a patron," urged Collinson, "eminent for his generosity and his noble spirit to promote every branch of natural history."

Peter Collinson must have felt a true sense of satisfaction in having found a solution at last to what he always considered the problem of poor Billy. Although he fussed, and scolded him, no man could have cared more for the difficult son of a friend he had never met.

A month later, Collinson's own "noble spirit" left his body.

John Bartram had great difficulty in absorbing the fact that Peter was dead. He had word of it from several sources: Linnaeus, Franklin, Fothergill, the young Lord Petre, and Michael Collinson. About his son, Michael, Peter had once written to John that "he was happy to have a child of so agreeable a cast."

Now Michael sent word that his father had become critically ill with a kidney ailment while on a visit in Essex to the ninth Lord Petre, whose father had been his dear friend and John Bartram's first patron. Returning home to Mill Hill, which he called his "Sweet & Calm old Mansion," he had remained philosophical as always. "Few men have enjoyed life more or been more exempt from pain or disease," he told his son. "And now that it has come so late in life, I am thankful to Providence that He has preserved me so long."

John Fothergill, ready to take up the plant, seed, and letter exchange where Collinson left off, wrote: "I owe much of my intimacy with the several branches of natural history to my deceased friend . . . His diligence and economy of time was such that, though he never appeared to be in a hurry, he maintained an extensive correspondence with great punctuality; acquainting the learned and ingenious in distant parts of the globe with the discoveries and improvements in natural history in this country . . . For my part I yet feel that in him I have lost a Friend who valued my happiness little less than his own."

John Bartram and his son Billy sat in the summerhouse near their cider press on the edge of the Schuylkill. The death of Collinson had plunged John into a protracted state of depression. "I never heard his voice nor saw his face, yet I loved him as much as my half brother William, perhaps more." It was a source of continuing regret to him that

Bartram to rescue his son, whose pride, obviously, would not allow him to make such a plea himself. I laid stress upon the forlorn state of this worthy and ingenious lad, who could prosper in a suitable environment but cannot prosper here. He is a passing fine artist; I have seen his work. But he has had discouragements enough to break the spirits of any man, and has been exposed to more difficulties than those whose crimes drive them to exile. All of this I wrote to Mr. Bartram."

James Grant sat silent for a moment. Then he said, "You did well, Henry. His father would want to know that; he has even gone so far as to ask me to find it out, as I told you. But let us hope that Billy, with his artless pride, never discovers what you have written."

It was Henry Laurens's turn to sit silent. He set down his punch cup on the silver tray and looked out across the acres of fertile indigo, upon which the sun was casting its last rays. "Indeed, Your Excellency," he said at last, "it was Billy who begged me to write it."

The next fall found Billy back at Kingsessing. He took a job as a day laborer on a nearby farm, as he had done before, and it seemed to him as though his life had swung around in a kind of circle, with all that time in between and nothing accomplished. He was twenty-eight years old, he told himself, and what had he done with his life? His youth was over; one failure had followed another, and here he was back home again, haying on the Schuylkill. He spent his days working as hard as his strength and energy would allow, and he tried not to think too much about the diaster at Picolata, which had been far more crushing to him than any of his other failures.

His family and friends were also deeply concerned by

what Peter Collinson had termed "William's unsteady conduct." It was indicative of Collinson's concern that he called him "William" instead of "Billy."

"Nothing but marrying will settle him," he wrote to John. "With a prudent, discreet woman, he may return to Florida, and amend his conduct." Typically, in the eagerness of his conviction, he had gone on to describe this woman as "such as knows how to share the toils as well as the comforts of a married state. If this is not done," he had added direfully, "he'll fall into the snares of a loose, unlawful way of life, from whence no good can come, but much evil and inconvenience."

In July of 1768, Peter Collinson wrote still another letter. In it he recounted that Lady William Henry Cavendish Bentinck, the Duchess of Portland, had dined with him. This in itself would hardly have been remarkable. The reason for the letter was to inform John and Billy that he had shown Her Highness a parcel of Billy's drawings which had arrived that very morning, and that the duchess had been delighted.

"So great was the deception, it being candlelight," Collinson described the scene, that they had disputed for some time whether the pictures were engravings or drawings. The duchess's delight was such that she forwarded twenty guineas to Billy with an order for "all Land, River and your sea Shells, from the very least to the greatest . . . not be crowded and most carefully done."

Finally, Peter Collinson found yet another patron for Billy, a man who would influence, aid, and ultimately alter and conserve the river of his life. "This morning," Peter wrote to John Bartram, "Dr. Fothergill came and breakfasted here. As I am thoughtful how to make Billy's ingenuity turn to some advantage, I bethought of showing the Doctor his last elegant performance. He deservedly admired them . . ."

John Fothergill was born in Yorkshire in 1712 of a Quaker

neither man had ever crossed the ocean to meet the other. "Had I not been so slow in recovering from my Florida fever, I might have managed to bear my journal and thy drawings to England myself. Now it is too late."

Billy, who often believed that his own life had been nothing but "might-haves," looked down at the gray river slipping softly by and reminded his father of something. "Does thee not remember what Mr. Collinson remarked to thee when thee was in distress about the abdication of Pitt? He urged, 'Don't sink and be lost in doleful dumps.' Imagine, Father, that he is saying it still."

Almost in his seventieth year, John felt far less sturdy and robust than he had before. He knew that he had undertaken his last extended journey. But he worked daily in his garden and it flourished. He prayed that the Creator would grant him at least a few more years for botanizing, both for the King and for himself and his family.

"And we still have Dr. Fothergill," Billy was saying.

"We still have Fothergill," repeated John. He squinted at the river as if looking down the road to the future and trying to determine whether John Fothergill might become to Billy what Peter Collinson had been to Billy's father.

CHAPTER 5

RETURN TO
THE ST. JOHNS

"Time is a river of passing events."
Marcus Aurelius

It hardly seemed possible to Billy that he was standing once more on the shores of that Georgia river where, eight years earlier, his father had discovered the "curious shrub" that he had not seen before or since. They had learned the name of the river; it was the Altamaha, or "Alatamaha," as they called it. But the mysterious tree had no name. When Billy had set sail from Philadelphia a month before, one of the last things his father had urged him to do was to look and see if the lost shrub still stood.

And here it is, thought Billy, breaking off a few leaves and placing them in his notebook, and here am I. The scene, although basically the same, was altered. Where it had been October, with the leaves aflame and the sky a burnished blue, it was now April, and a fine driving rain, like little thin needles, came from the slaty clouds. The trees, many just barely leafed-out, stood in their palest green. Through the autumn's fallen foliage the early flowers of the shade poked out, violets and bloodroot and anemones. Dark streams, bearing the winter's melted snow, crashed in white bubbles on the mossy rocks. Wrens and warblers trilled in the cleft ravines or in the dripping forest canopy.

Billy remembered vaguely, 'I was unhappy here before.' It was strange how little of that he actually did remember. 'I went to look for ducks on the river,' he recalled, 'and when I returned, my father shouted out to me that he had found a new tree. Its blooming time was over, but it had not yet formed ripe seeds. Now its blooming time has not yet begun. So I must come again,' said Billy.

He would hardly have recognized the anxious and tormented young man that he had been before. So much had happened since; so much of good and bad had left its mark on him. He had grown to manhood, he sensed, later than his contemporaries; he had been a dreamer and a procrastinator far longer than most. At thirty-four, by eighteenth-century standards, he was beginning late indeed on what he felt was his life's commitment.

So there, beside what he thought of as his father's tree, he prayed briefly to his Creator to be granted enough time to do what he had to do.

It was understandable that time, or the potential lack of it, was much on his mind. He had been deeply shaken by the death of his Uncle William three years before. Later he was to write that his uncle was "beloved & esteemed for his patriotic Virtues," and that "His House was open & his Table free, to his neighbour, the oppressed & the Stranger." Apart from his own sorrow, he had been tortured by the thought of Mary's. Although he seldom heard from her, he had not ceased thinking of the idyllic days spent in her company.

He thought of them particularly while toiling in the shop of his brother-in-law, George, for whom, after all, he had had to go to work. George, whose last name was also Bar-

tram, was a Scotsman who had married Billy's sister, Ann.
They ran a business which John felt was a more suitable
place for Billy than the neighbor's fields, where he had been
employed off and on as a laborer.

Thus for the third time in his life Billy found himself
confined behind a new counter, and for the third time the
figuring and the responsibilities proved too much for him to
cope with. In any case, suddenly and unexpectedly he left
not only the shop but his family too, apparently in a moment
of great stress, even terror.

He fled to Ashwood as though drawn there, to the big
empty house haunted by memories. Eventually he let his
father know where he was, and that long-suffering man replied, in the April of 1771, that it was a satisfaction to hear
from Billy since the family had "never heard the least account of thee after thee left us so unnaturally."

He went on to add, with a patience not unmixed with
resignation: "We have prevailed on thy Creditors to take one
hundred pounds ready cash & give a full discharge forever &
George Bartram hath paid in on my account; he also paid
that troublesome man who threatened thee on his own account, I think the day before thee went away."

"All thy papers," his kind father continued, "is to be sent
according to thy desire. We are as well as when thee left us,
but my sight is much worse . . . I expect thy brothers will
write more fully; it is with difficulty that I can see to write at
all . . . Thy mother joyns with me in love to thee . . . &
remain thy loving parents."

However disappointed and perplexed John might be with
his wandering and unpredictable son, he never withheld one
jot of his love or the liberal expression of it.

A few months later he sent another message. Billy had
apparently conceived the notion of returning to St. Augustine to attempt once more what he had failed to do the last
time, and achieve his dream of growing indigo on the San

Juan. The year before, over sixteen thousand pounds of it had been shipped to England, and the textile industry there was eager for more. John received the idea with typical dismay.

"We are surprised at thy wild notion of going to Augustine," he wrote in his firm and steady hand. "Indeed I don't intend to have any more of my estate spent there or to ye southerd upon any pretence whatsoever. I think it is much better for thee to come home & dwell amongst thy relations & friends who I doubt not will endeavor & put thee in A way of profitable business if thee will take their advice & be industrious & carefull. My eye sight is gone very dim & I have thrown off all plantation business to John & we live with him . . . mother & John & benny remember their love for thee & I remain thy loving father John Bartram."

No doubt had Billy not suffered and failed in so many of those "profitable" businesses, he would have found it nearly impossible to resist such an outpouring of love and reasoning. Still, he lingered on in indecision at Ashwood, until something finally occurred to send him hastening home.

Dr. John Fothergill, the London physician and friend of Peter Collinson, to whom Peter had, almost as his last act, shown and praised Billy's drawings, all at once appeared like a *deus ex machina.*

To John Bartram he wrote that he had promised Peter he would do something to help the boy, as it was indeed a pity that "such a genius should sink under distress." Billy had sent Fothergill a few drawings of turtles and mollusks, although not as many as had been hoped for. His hand, though, was "a good one; and by attention and care may become excellent."

Fothergill then proposed to sponsor and finance an expedition for Billy.

What he really wanted was to have Billy travel north to

Canada to discover and collect for English gardens "the more hardy plants such as will bear our winters without much shelter." He did not seem to share the average Englishman's fascination with the American subtropics. Perhaps he felt that Florida had already been adequately reported upon by John.

But Billy's heart was set on returning to Florida, and that was where he was bound to go. So Dr. Fothergill conceded and sent him minute instructions about the methods of collecting and preserving plant specimens and seeds, and the safest way to ship them. He also instructed him concerning exactly the sort of plants to look for, not neglecting shells and fossils and other natural objects of interest. In closing, he reminded him to remember his Maker, and to be much alone.

Billy, who felt that much of his life had already been spent in loneliness, had to smile at this.

John Fothergill also wrote to an acquaintance of his, and presumably of Alexander Garden's and Henry Laurens's, a Charleston physician named Lionel Chalmers, who was in a position to introduce Billy to helpful people in the southeast and also to act as his financial agent. Billy was to be given fifty pounds a year, with a ten-guinea advance to help him prepare for his journey. In addition, he was to be paid for his individual drawings. Formerly Billy had been reluctant and confused about placing a value on his work; he had little or no idea how much his pictures might be worth or what price they might bring. Now Dr. Fothergill, his patron, believed that Dr. Chalmers could help him with this dilemma and also forward funds to him in the wilderness. These letters crossed the ocean in October 1772.

On April 1 of the next year, Billy was at Dr. Chalmers's house in Charleston. He had sailed from Philadelphia on March 20.

On April 7, Lionel Chalmers wrote to John Bartram that

he had paid Billy the ten guineas. Considerately, he added: "But as that sum, with all his Frugality, would not go far, I desired at the end of six months or sooner, that he would draw on me for £25 more, which I would Pay, as well as the remaining £25 at the Year's End; for it could not be expected that he could travel & maintain himself for 12 months on the first Ten Guineas Dr. Fothergill desired might be paid him."

Dr. Chalmers was anxious that William, as he called him, waste no time to "do something to please Dr. Fothergill . . . for the season for Flowers will soon be over."

That Lionel Chalmers took a personal interest not only in handling funds for Billy but also in his work itself, even so far as to offer helpful criticism, is shown further on in this thoughtfully written letter: "He certainly has a good notion of Painting; he might take an excellent Representation of Things, were he more exact in his colourings after Nature, which, from a sample he gave me of the Starry Anise Flower, I had to caution him to be."

The "Starry Anise Flower" was the plant that Billy first discovered on the trip with his father, returning home on the San Juan River.

"A painted Finch which flew on board of the Vessel in his Passage hither, he painted beautifully," Dr. Chalmers continued, with no idea, of course, what that bird might mean to Billy. "On the whole, I doubt not, he will fully answer Dr. Fothergill's expectation, to make it answer well for himself, considering he is to be paid separately for all his Drawings."

Then, in a revealing postscript, a point was made that many must have agreed with, whether they said so or not. "Your son," Chalmers added, after his signature, "has all the Requisites & Application to Researches of this soil, that his Father had before him—and indeed it surprises me, that you should not have encouraged this genius of his as a Naturalist sooner; for, tho' you endeavour'd to curb it by putting him to a Mercht etc., yet Nature prevailed so far as to disqualify him from Pursuits of this sort. On the whole, John Bartram had a son, who I hope will perpetuate both his Father's and his own Name, for the advancement of Natural Philosophy, as well as of Science in general."

With these gently chiding and prophetic words the letter ended.

It was not until April 1774, a whole year later, that Billy finally found himself in Florida. During that year he had traveled throughout Georgia, calling upon people to whom he had been given letters of introduction by Dr. Chalmers, "a gentleman of eminence in his profession and public employments," Billy wrote later, who "received me with perfect politeness, and, on every occasion, treated me with friendship." Among those to whom Lionel Chalmers introduced him by letter was Governor Wright at Savannah, where Billy arrived by ship from Charleston in twenty-four hours. It being still early spring, he was eager to press further south. "His Excellency," he recorded, "received me with great politeness, shewed me every mark of esteem and regard, and furnished me with letters to the principle inhabitants of the state, which were of great service to me."

Billy had obviously come a long way since the days when he had been too shy to speak to customers and urge them to buy, the days when he had trailed his father about his garden and on his journeys, and listened diffidently to the words of Franklin and Colden and Kalm.

Near the settlement of Darien, on the banks of the Altamaha, Billy arrived at the plantation of the McIntosh family, whose Scottish ancestors had been among the first colonists of Georgia under General Oglethorpe. Presenting his credentials, Billy was made instantly at home, indeed a part of the family. When he finally left, the eldest son, John McIntosh, accompanied him as "a very agreeable companion through a long and toilsome journey of near a thousand miles."

But all through his Georgia days, Billy was consumed with his longing to continue to Florida. Many obstacles stood in the way: there were countless plants to be collected and detailed drawings to be made for Dr. Fothergill; there was his illness with a "violent Fever" at the McIntosh plantation. "We are, all of us, subject to crosses and disappointments, but more especially the traveller," he wrote, "and when they surprise us, we frequently become restless and impatient under them: but let us . . . learn wisdom and understanding in the economy of nature, and be seriously attentive to the divine monitor within."

He had learned one of the great principles of life: to flow with the river of time and events, and not to fight the current. A century later Emerson was to entreat much the same thing.

So Billy had progressed from the impatient and careless boy that he had been; so his sensitive nature and character developed and expressed itself. The years spent on the banks of the Schuylkill and traveling with his father and alone had played their part in molding the form that now emerged.

He heard only infrequently from Kingsessing, and as usual wrote even less often. Letters from Dr. Fothergill reached him now and then, forwarded by Dr. Chalmers. In September his patron had written to remind him to keep a journal in which he should make notes of the places where he found his plants growing, whether "under shade or in the open country," and also of the kinds of soil and any "remarkable animals" he observed.

Billy also received the news that autumn that George Edwards, to whom he had sent his earliest bird pictures and who had encouraged him to draw more, had died in July at the age of eighty.

"It was now about the middle of April," in 1774. Billy had

bought a small sailboat for three guineas, and "continually impelled by a restless spirit of curiosity," set sail with a fair wind up the San Juan River from the ferry crossing of Cowford, now Jacksonville. He was alone. His promised companion, "though stouter and heartier" than Billy, had apparently had misgivings about the Indians he might meet at the trading posts and preferred to remain in the comparative security of the plantations.

Billy professed not to regret his solitary state, and indeed he was freer to pursue and discover the "original productions of nature" that he, his father, Dr. Fothergill, and much of the aware and thoughtful world were concerned with. "My chief happiness," he felt then, "consisted in tracing and admiring the infinite power, majesty and perfection of the great Almighty Creator." It was understandable that he was not entirely unwilling to part with his proposed companion.

In truth, he did not feel himself alone. Where Mary had traveled with him in his heart on his other southern journey, surely his father's spirit and influence must have accompanied him on this river trip that they had once undertaken together. Much must have looked familiar, and with the previous voyage constantly in his mind, these places doubtless assumed that luminous quality and added dimension that revisited sites acquire.

And yet how different it all must have seemed from that other time on the river, when there had been his father and a guide-and-hunter and a rower-and-cook. Passing Fort Picolata, Billy could not resist going ashore to see the site of that colorful congress with the governor and the Creeks. But where once there had been banners and the firing of guns, officers resplendent in uniform and Indians in paint and feathers, all was emptiness. The old Spanish fortress had been dismantled and deserted. Standing again on that swampy point of land where he had killed the rattlesnake, and seeing the ancient fort now so changed, Billy must have had a vivid and graphic revelation of the passing of time, flowing through his life even faster than the running river before him.

And when he passed the sandy strip where the rains and tides had washed away his precious plants, could he have helped wondering at the fluctuations of his fortunes and pondering what lay ahead, and whether success, or at least fulfillment, might ever come to him?

As with his father before him, nothing along the way escaped his notice or his admiration. "How glorious the Palm!" he wrote, "how majestically stands the Laurel, its head forming a perfect cone!" "Keeping along the West or Indian shore, I saw basking, on the sedgy banks, numbers of alligators, some of them of an enormous size." Billy acknowledged that he used the terms "alligator" and "crocodile" indiscriminately, "alligator" being, he believed, "the country name."

The great reptiles fascinated him, and he described their uncommon abundance, their ferocious fighting which boiled the water's surface, and their dreaded roaring and bellowing that filled the air and shook the ground for miles around, shores and forests alike resounding with the "horrid combat."

By the end of April, Billy had reached another familiar landmark, James Spalding's Lower Store on the shores of Lake George. He was treated with "great politeness . . . the utmost civility and friendship," by the agent there. And so it was not until the middle of May, having in the meantime made a journey west to the Alachua trading post, that Billy set out again up the San Juan.

Three years earlier, Bernard Romans, a well-known civil engineer of the time, had started an official survey of the river, but he never reached its swampy, grassy source. Fifty miles from the spot where John's "battoe" had run into the sand and Billy had leapt out to stand at the head of navigation, Romans abandoned the project.

When the French Huguenot, Jean Ribault, discovered his "River of May," he found its country "the fairest, frutefullest and pleasantest of all the worlde, habonding in honney, veneson, wildfoule, forestes, woodes of all sortes, palme trees, cipers, ceders, bayes . . . okes and other trees that be of wonderfull greatnes and height."

"The faire medowes," he added, "are full of herons, corleux, bitterns, mallardes, egretes, woodkockes and all kine of small birds."

Billy saw them too. They adorn the pages of his journals. There were the owls, whose "whooping" awakened and terrified him, and the "sonorous" savanna (or sandhill) crane, a flock of which he observed soaring and wheeling, ascending in spiral circles, rising and falling together "as one bird." He plainly heard their feathers, as they beat the dense air, "creak as the joints or working of a vessel in a tempestuous sea."

One day Billy tasted "this fowl dressed for supper and it made excellent soup; nevertheless," he wrote, "as long as I can get any other necessary food I shall prefer his seraphic music in the ethereal skies."

Fortunately, other food was plentiful. Sometimes Billy broiled a trout with oil and "the lively juice of oranges, a valuable substitute for vinegar." Once two large bears, attracted by the fragrance of the cooking, approached, but they did not attempt to molest him. Nothing disturbed him, he claimed, but "the whooping of owls, screaming of bitterns, or the wood-rats running amongst the leaves."

Whether to eat, watch, or draw, fish always interested him. He hardly knew whether to believe his own eyes when he saw "that the river (in this place) from shore to shore, and perhaps near half a mile above and below . . . appeared to be one solid bank of fish, of various kinds, pushing through this narrow pass of St. Juans." In the same place, "the alligators were in such incredible numbers, and so close together from shore to shore, that it would have been easy to have walked across on their heads, had the animals been harmless.

"What expressions can sufficiently declare the shocking scene that for some minutes continued, whilst this mighty army of fish were forcing the pass? During this attempt, thousands, I may say hundreds of thousands of them were caught and swallowed by the devouring alligators."

Of all the fish he saw, the yellow bream, or sunfish, seems to have been his favorite. "What a most beautiful creature is this fish before me!" he recorded joyfully, "gliding to and fro, and figuring in the still clear waters, with his orient attendants and associates." And he sketched and painted many breams with sparkling detail.

It is obvious that Billy was happy on his St. Johns journey. In all his notes his delight is evident. "Having agreeably diverted away the intolerable heats of sultry noon in fruitful fragrant groves, with renewed vigor I again resume my sylvan pilgrimage . . . Before night . . . at a charming Orange grove bluff . . . I had time to get some fine trout for supper and joyfully return to my camp.

"How harmonious and soothing is this native sylvan music now at still evening! inexpressibly tender are the responsive cooings of the innocent dove . . . the shades of silent night are made more cheerful . . . What a beautiful display of vegetation is here before me! . . . what can equal the rich golden flowers . . . which ornament the banks of yon serpentine rivulet, meandering over the meadows."

Billy Bartram, rescued from the prison of schoolhouse and store, from the burdens of the anxiety about him of his family and their friends, and from the torments of an unfulfilled love affair, certainly felt and revealed an exuberance and natural surprise which seldom, over the years of traveling, ever left him. Nor was his appreciation naïve or childish, born solely of liberation. Doubtless it was engendered by his father and by his father's remarkable acquaintances, whom Billy did not forget, and particularly by his God. Alone in the wilderness of East Florida, he did not feel himself alone, "but under the care of the Almighty, and protected by the invisible hand of my guardian angel."

One night, a "rapacious" wolf stole the fish Billy had caught and hung on a branch to enjoy for breakfast. "How much easier and more eligible it might have been," he wrote, continuing in his enchanted mood, "for him to have leaped upon my breast in the dead of sleep, and torn my throat, which would have instantly deprived me of life."

The next day Billy came again upon the very spot where, in late January eight years before, he had discovered the new plant of which his father had been so proud. Now he looked again at the yellow starry anise he had found and knew a sense of fresh contentment in the "alluring scene . . . The towering Magnolia itself a grove, and the exalted Palm, as if conscious of their transcendent glories."

He noted the crystal waters, with the "social prattling coot enrobed in blue, and the squealing water-hen." Above all else he loved the birds, and he recorded every kind he saw, making a "most complete and correct" list of some two hundred and fifteen species in all. Among them were the "curious and handsome bird, the people call them Snake Birds," which he doubted not but "if this bird had been an inhabitant of the Tiber in Ovid's days, it would have furnished him with a subject, for some beautiful and entertaining metamorphoses." Thus he revealed the reading that he too had done in Mr. Logan's collection and Mr. Franklin's new Library Company.

Besides the snakebird, Billy described the limpkin, called by the Indians "the crying bird" because of its blood-chilling, human-sounding wail; and the squadrons of white ibis, then named Spanish curlews; and the wood ibis, or stork, which years before Mark Catesby, the exploring English-man, had called the wood pelican. In their "pensive posture and solitary situation," Billy wrote, "they look extremely grave, sorrowful and melancholy, as if in deepest thought." He discovered the Florida, or scrub, jay and noted its differ-ence from the "great crested jay of Virginia."

It had been a long time ago that Billy Bartram had sat under the tulip tree in his father's garden and drawn the scarlet tanager on its nest, and a long time too since he had watched the phoebes with his cousin Mary on Moore's Creek Bridge, but he had never lost his particular love of birds or his patience and ability to observe them closely and describe them exactly.

Later it was said of him that he laid the foundations of American ornithology. In any case, he was the first native-born bird watcher to contribute reliable records and lists. Every page of his journals identifies him as a true product of his time. He did not care for simple listing and recording; he saw every plant and animal as a living individual in close relationship to its environment. In this sense, Billy and his father before him, who taught him, may be considered America's first ecologists.

His letters, however few, must have reassured John, who naturally worried about his son's safety, especially in Indian country. Dr. Fothergill wrote to John Bartram that Billy had sent him some "curious" dried plants and also some draw-ings, although not as many as Fothergill would have liked.

In this respect Billy had not changed. He still found it difficult to write and draw when all of a new out-of-doors was calling to him. Fothergill, financing Billy's trip, felt justified in complaining about the lack of drawings and com-munication in general. Hopefully he sent reams of paper to Billy, by way of Lionel Chalmers, and also the news that a fourth edition of John Bartram's *Description of East Florida,* first published in William Stork's *Account of East Florida,* had just been printed in London.

One fine evening in midsummer of that year, 1774, Billy, having moored his "bark" near a long point of flat rocks on Lake George, left his camping site and came upon the deserted plantation of Dr. Stork. There in the twilight, hearing the soft calling of the mourning doves and perhaps a chuck-will's-widow from an ancient grove, he had wandered beneath the gnarled, untended orange trees and seen the sweet-scented, night-blooming moonflower vine, "climbing and strolling on the shrubs and hedges."

How changed was the prospect from the way it had been on that first visit with his father, nearly ten years before. Then, having just been gained from the Indians, the land was extensively cleared, fenced, and planted by native laborers. William Stork had high hopes for a successful indigo business. In a formal petition to the King, he had offered to import workers from Germany, if the British government would donate one of His Majesty's sloops for the ocean voyage. Stork had suggested that the ship might be not one in present use but even one deemed "unfit for public service." It is hardly surprising that the petition was not granted.

Billy, then twenty-six, had been deeply impressed with the plantation. Perhaps he might also be able to have one, on a smaller scale at first, of course; then with acre on acre flourishing along the riverbank. So he remembered himself as a boy, and he smiled ruefully, dreaming as he walked through the old fields and the once-clipped hedges now burdened with moonflowers.

The next morning, continuing around the lake, he came to another "property of a British gentleman, but some years since vacated. A very spacious frame building was settling to

ILLUSTRATIONS

BALSAM PEAR, or African cucumber: edible orange fruit, yellow
seeds and bright crimson pulp

"PURPLE BERR'D BAY OF CAT[ESBY]," *Olea americana,*
a sweet-scented shrub; "RED SPARAW or Red bird of America
THE WILD CRAB OF NORTH CAROLINA 1772 WB"; fish
unidentified

"The HUMMINGBIRD   The Great STONE CRAB   A little SEA
SHELL   All from the Seacoast of Cape Fear No Carolina"

AMERICAN LOTUS. In the left foreground, the VENUS FLY-
TRAP and the GREAT BLUE HERON. Probably drawn during
a visit to Ashwood

Tab. I.

In the background, a seed pod of the AMERICAN LOTUS. In the foreground, a PITCHER PLANT, a LAND SNAIL, and a SCARLET SNAKE with a frog. Probably drawn in Brunswick County, North Carolina

Tab. II.

FRANKLINIA ALTAHAMA, a plant discovered by the Bartrams in Georgia and named for Benjamin Franklin. The flowers are white with a gold center

Franklinia

PHYSIC NUT. "The Indians carry the ripe frute with them when out on hunts supposing it to have the power of attracting deer. & so they call it the Physic Nut." Bird unidentified

Tab. 1.

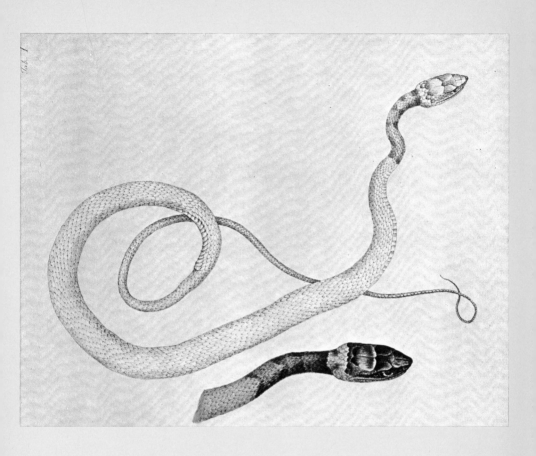

"GREAT SAVANAH CRANE.   Ash colour   the quill feathers dusky or black"

"THE GREAT MALLARD OF FLORIDA"

Tab. IV

"GREAT GOLDEN SPECKLED BREAM of St. John. E[as]t
Florida   W.B.   1774"

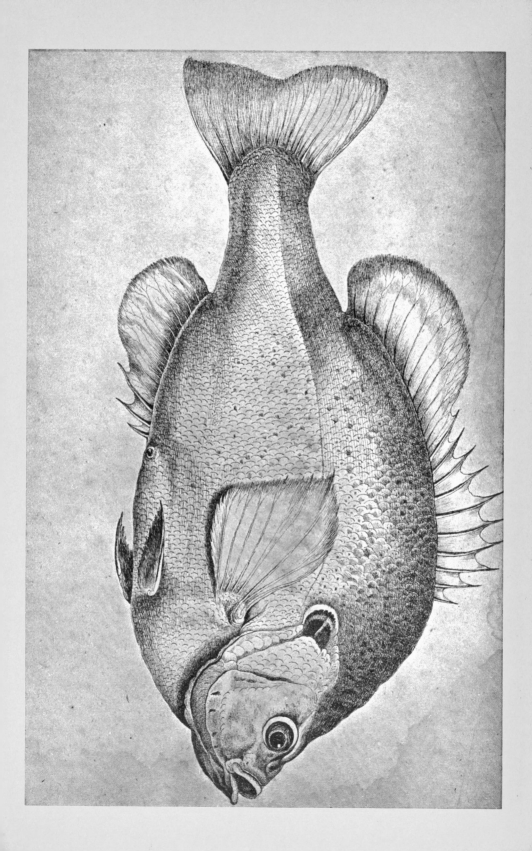

Fig. 1 GERARDIA, narrow, dark-green leaves, rose-colored flowers
Fig. 2 WILLOW PRIMROSE, yellow flowers which wilt in the sun
Fig. 3 BUTTERWORT, "various col'd flowers, blue, Yellow, white & c"

Fig. 1.

2

3

Primula aurea & Wa.

MORNING GLORY (pale rose) entwined with a WILD LIME,
or tallow nut. The nut is "of the consistency and taste of the sweet
Almond, but more oily and very much like hard tallow"

Fig. 1

2.

Fig. 1   "PAPAW APPLE ANONA. Flowers large & white.
        Fruite when ripe is of an agreeable fragrance well tasted, &
        are commonly eaten"
Fig. 2   "ANONA. The flower & fruite much like the preceding
        species, the petalae are long narrow of a pale purple"

Tab.XVII.

Fig. 2.

Fig. 1.

"The ALEGATOR of St. Johns"

Fig. 1   "Represents the action of this terrable monster when they
         bellow in the Spring Season. they force the water out of their
         throat which falls from their mouth like a Cataract & a steam
         or vapour from their Nostrals like smoke"

Fig. 2   "Represents them rising up out of the water when they devour
         the fish &c. . . . Journal up St. Johns River E[as]t Florida"

Tab. III

Fig. 1.

Fig. 2.

The Aligator of St Johns

the ground and mouldering to earth; here are very extensive old fields, where were growing the West Indian or perennial Cotton and Indigo, which had been cultivated here, and some scattered remains of the ancient Orange groves, which had been left standing at the clearing of the plantation."

How eerie it must have been to see the ruins, particularly when Billy could remember the plantations as they had been only so recently, active and flourishing. He was also "affected with extreme regret" by the clearing itself. New planters under the British government had apparently "indiscreetly" cut down hundreds of acres of trees to "make room for the Indigo, Cotton, Corn, Batatas, &. or as they say, to extirpate the musquitoes, alledging that groves near their dwellings are haunts and shelters for those persecuting insects; some plantations have not a single tree standing . . . having no lofty cool grove . . . to shade and protect them, exhibiting a mournful, sallow countenance."

As well as being one of the first American ecologists, William Bartram may well have been one of the first conservationists too.

Aside from his "extreme regret at beholding the destruction and devastation," Billy continued to be content with his travels. When he arrived at the Upper and Lower Stores, and at other trading posts, he brought with him "valuable collections" for ultimate shipment to Dr. Fothergill.

In all, he had made over one hundred drawings, including some which were roughly sketched on the backs of others. Among them were "Wattoola, the Great Savannah Crane . . . Ash colour, the quill feathers dusky or black." The bird had been shot for a "pilloe," but before it was dressed, Billy made a lively representation of it stepping off across the flatland, not forgetting to include the bald cypress by the riverbank, where a sailing ship is waiting and an antlered deer looks on. Nothing escaped him. And what the scene did not provide, his memory or imagination did.

Of course, he sent his drawings of the breams: the great black, of which he remarked that the eyes were "large and black with red flashes or streams like fire"; the red-bellied, a "beautiful large River fish"; and his favorite, the yellow, about which he wrote to his patron: "This is an excellent fish of E. Florida. Some of them are near a foot in length, they have a very large mouth. He is generally of a rich yellow or gold color with dark flesh col'd Fins. The head & upper side darkest, but everywhere powdered and freckled with green, purple, gold & silver . . . This is a very bold ravenous fish, like the leopard secretes himself in some hole or dark retreat & rushes out on a sudden snapping up the smaller fish passing by."

He painted the green heron foraging along the riverbank. The "Little green Bittern," Billy called it, "represented here of natural size and colour." The Andromeda, a "Noble ever-green Shrub," Billy went on to describe beneath his handsome drawing in a penmanship surprisingly neat and regular for one of so artistic a temperament: "These extraordinary appearances of beautifull Flowers are more like fiction or the exertions of an eregular fancy than of Nature."

He drew the cardinal, "the Crested Red Bird of Florida, or Virginia Nightingale." Shells, snakes, frogs, and tortoises were not neglected; neither were alligators. A dramatic portrayal of "The Alegator of St. Johns" has been called "the most famous and most important drawing executed by Bartram."

This illustration contains two depictions of alligators. One shows the reptile rising from the water to devour a fish; the other "Represents the action of this terrable monster when they bellow in the Spring Season. They force the water out of their throat which falls from their mouth like a Cataract & a steam or vapour from their Nostrals like smoke."

Billy believed that the bellow of the alligator prophesied rain. "About noon the weather became extremely sultry," he wrote on a late summer's day on the St. Johns, "not a breath of wind stirring, hazy or cloudy, and very distant thunder, which is answered by the crocodiles, sure presage of a storm!"

And a storm indeed it was. Billy, always fascinated by these phenomena, missed no detail. "How purple and fiery appeared the tumultuous clouds! swiftly ascending or darting from the horizon upwards; they seemed to oppose and dash against each other, the skies appeard streaked with blood or purple flame overhead, the flaming lightning streaming and darting about in every direction around, seems to fill the world with fire; whilst the heavy thunder keeps the earth in a constant tremor . . . the rain came down with such rapidity and fell in such quantities, that every object was totally obscured, excepting the continual streams or rivers of lightning, pouring from the clouds; all seemed a frightful chaos."

Hundreds of miles away, in the cool springtime of a northern colony, another kind of chaos erupted. In the Province of Massachusetts Bay, at a country town whose name meant peace, some farmers left their plows standing in the fields, and on April 19, 1775, they took up arms at last against the red-coated soldiers of the mother country and "fired the shot heard round the world."

It was heard in Lexington, where shots had already been fired, and it was heard in Boston. It was heard in Philadelphia less than a week later, and in Richmond on April 30.

Billy Bartram had left his East Florida the fall before and in South Carolina had prepared and shipped his specimens and drawings. He had also discussed his future travel plans, "agreeable to Dr. Fothergill's instructions and the council and advice of Dr. Chalmers of Charleston, with other gentlemen of that city, eminent for the promotion of science and encouraging merit and industry."

It was Billy's dream to proceed west into the Cherokee country, and from there even farther west to the nation and regions of the Creek Indians, and perhaps to the great Mississippi itself. On April 22 he set forth on horseback. By the time the news of Concord Bridge reached Charleston, Billy had already ridden as far as Augusta and beyond, and he was preparing to cross the Savannah River. The embattled farmers' shot had not yet been heard in his green world.

CHAPTER 6

INDIAN TRAILS

"I am as free as Nature first made man,
Ere the base laws of servitude began,
When wild in woods the noble savage ran."

John Dryden

The mountains were named for the smokelike mists, spiraling up from the valleys and the densely wooded slopes, concealing the skyline. Frequent rains enhanced the image. Wispy halos clung to the domes, rounded by aeons of weather. The Great Smokies were millions of years old when the first Rockies thrust their peaks from the flat western plains.

Uncounted centuries of precipitation, frost, and wind and dark streams swelled by melting snow and summer storms had carved away at the jutting land mass. Mountain building, begun when there was little if any life on earth, gave way to mountain carving, as the earth's crust settled and natural erosion softened the contours of the Appalachian range. What were once jagged, treeless crests became undulating horizons, blending in the distance from green to blue to violet, feathery in the leafing-out of May.

When Billy Bartram looked on this ancient scene in that historic spring of 1775, what amazed him most was the feeling of mobility and transience that the landscape presented as the passing clouds and cloud shadows appeared to attach themselves to the trees and seemed to move the hills across the sky.

Actually, the mountaintops had not always been so feathery and green. Once, when they had towered some five times higher than in colonial times, they must have had a true timberline, above which, on gray rock precipices, lichens spread out their windowpane frost patterns, and tiny, colorful, fragrant Alpine flowers blossomed under the ice.

As the great glaciers plowed and poured down from the north over other mountains and valleys, they violently uprooted trees and pushed before them seeds of many kinds with, always racing on ahead, a terrified, fleeing population of wild animals.

When the ice sheet finally melted, the seeds and roots, frozen and preserved, were able to lodge in whatever earth they found. The glaciers, retreating, left their deposits of soil, and the vegetation was quick to take over. Instead of moving north, latitudinally, to their optimum microclimate, many species moved up the mountainsides, altitudinally. Some, over hundreds of centuries, adapted to their new environment, as transplanted life always endeavors to do. Thus it was that Billy saw, stranded on the misty summits of Carolina, hardwoods and conifers that belonged more to the woods of Cadwallader Colden and Jared Eliot than to this place.

And it was then that he sensed that what he really saw was a sort of forest museum, one small preserved remnant of the primeval stands that had flourished, long before the dinosaurs, over vast sections of both hemispheres.

High-altitude forests usually contain few varieties of trees. Along the mossy trails six thousand feet above sea level, Billy marked mostly spruce and fir. Farther below he had ridden through groves of soaring oaks and white pines with trunks more than ten feet in circumference.

"I now enter upon the verge of the dark forest, charming solitude!" he wrote, "between the stately columns of the superb forest trees." There he came upon the "unparallelled cascade of Falling Creek, rolling and leaping off the rocks, which uniting below, spread a broad, glittering sheet of crystal waters. . . . I here seated myself on the moss clad rocks, under the shade of spreading trees and floriferous fragrant shrubs, in full view of the cascades."

Thus, while Philadelphia and Charleston buzzed with the news from Concord and the Second Continental Congress met hurriedly not far from Kingsessing, with Franklin, John Hancock, Patrick Henry, and a young Virginia burgess named Jefferson in attendance, and while General Washington prepared to leave the Congress and take command of the Army of the United Colonies, Billy sat on his mossy stone, admiring the "vegetable beauties" of rhododendron, and *Kalmia latifolia* (named for his Finnish friend), and particularly the azalea, "that suddenly opening to view from dark shades, we are alarmed with the apprehension of the hills being set on fire."

"I left the stream for a little while," Billy wrote on in the journal that Dr. Fothergill had urged him to keep, "passing swiftly and foaming over its rocky bed, lashing the steep craggy banks, and then suddenly sunk from my sight, murmuring hollow and deep under the rocky surface of the ground." He had never lost his fascination with underground springs and rivers, born that day on the St. Johns when, with his father, he had watched through transparent waters a plume of bubbles churning and boiling up from the white sand.

Leaving the stream, he rode through green fields, "parterres, vistas, and verdant swelling knolls, profusely productive of flowers and fragrant strawberries, their rich juice dying my horses feet and ancles. These swelling hills, the prolific beds on which the towering mountains repose, seem to have been the common situations of the towns of the ancients, as appear from the remaining ruins of them yet to be seen; and the level rich vale and meadows in front, their planting grounds."

For Billy Bartram had not come to the Great Smokies simply for exploring and plant-hunting in the mountains. He had a special mission to the Cherokee Nation there.

What originally brought the Cherokees to the hills and river bottoms of this part of the Appalachian chain, and when they arrived, is as shrouded in myth and fable as the mountaintops are shrouded in mist. The Indians, descendants presumably of those wanderers from Asia who made their way across the Bering Strait when it was dry land, came from the west, or "the sunsetting" as they called it. Following the animal herds that they hunted, the nomads proceeded down the new continent. Into the deeply wooded wilderness they roamed, leaving a trail of arrowheads and spear points, until they settled at last where the land looked good to them. There, in fertile valleys, they fashioned implements of clay, cultivated maize, danced for rain or corn, feasted for moon and fire, worshipped their elemental gods, and built and left the ceremonial mounds that Billy called "magnificent monuments."

Ten years before, in that memorable summer of 1765 when Billy had accompanied his father to the Florida territory and the congress at Fort Picolata, he had met, along with Governor Grant, a Captain John Stuart, in charge of Indian affairs in the south. Billy would never forget the sight of those two men, elegant in their uniforms and decorations, riding on their equally elegantly decorated horses down that sandy road.

Captain Stuart had come from England to Georgia under

General Oglethorpe and had almost immediately established a unique rapport with the Indians. The Cherokees particularly admired him, and called him "Bushyhead" because of his mass of red hair. It is said that there still resides, somewhere in the hills, a Cherokee family, descended from the captain, bearing the name of Bushyhead.

In Charleston, in preparation for his trip to the Smokies, Billy had gone to call upon Captain Stuart, seeking information, letters of introduction, and encouragement for his solitary venture into the Cherokee Nation. The information and letters were willingly given; the encouragement was not. The old warrior, map maker, negotiator, and superintendent, over seventy now, felt that it was far from wise for the young, naïve, and inexperienced Billy to go alone among a people who had learned to mistrust and dislike the white man, and who allowed only traders with permits from the Crown to pass.

Stuart himself had had a narrow escape from death at the hands of the Indians during the Cherokee War, his life having been saved at the last minute by Chief Ata-kullakulla during the massacre and retreat from Fort Loudon in 1760. The chief, whom the white men called the Little Carpenter for the way he had built his nation, valued Stuart for his fairness to his tribe. On the ruse of taking him hunting, he led him through the forest and set him on his way home.

What the captain sought to impress upon this idealistic son of the eminent John Bartram was that to ride into Indian country at this time was foolhardy in the extreme. Most Cherokees, he tried to tell him, more than merely disliked a stranger; they killed him.

Billy pondered these warnings, turning them over in his mind. Each time he came to the same conclusion. All men were his brothers; he was stranger to no man. He would go into the Cherokee Nation as a friend and return with friends of his own.

It soon became apparent that none of the frontiersmen he met along the way were willing to accompany this brother-to-all-men into the Indian realms. Guides were promised but did not appear; transitory companions lost heart or courage and left him. Alone then, as he had journeyed before, he encountered the uncertain beauties of that Appalachian spring.

"May we suppose that mankind feel in their hearts, a predeliction for the society of each other?" he wrote wistfully in his notebook, remembering the pleasant social life of the Charleston he had so recently forsaken: the teas, the balls, the receptions in walled gardens, the long conversations with compatible acquaintances of his father and Mr. Franklin. He could not, in fact, resist comparing his present situation "in some degree to Nebuchadnezzar's, when expelled from the society of men, and constrained to roam in the mountains and wilderness, there to herd and feed with the wild beasts of the forest."

That there was also pleasant society in the wilderness, Billy had already inadvertently discovered. While riding through a forest bordering on a meandering river valley where flocks of wild turkeys strolled and deer pranced in the flowery meadows, he had observed a party of Cherokee girls, "tall, slim, and of a graceful figure," gathering strawberries and bathing in the stream.

Their delight in the fragrant fruit and in the breeze and water, their berry-stained lips and cheeks, indeed the whole "enchanting scene of primitive innocence," so overwhelmed Billy that he attempted to join them. For his daring he was presented with a basket of berries and a close look at their "captivating features and manners." But he was, in spite of his naïveté, worldly enough to realize that the white man, however hopeful and sanguine, had not and perhaps might never have a place in "these Elysian fields."

Could he possibly have made a mistake, he sometimes wondered in his aloneness, in venturing so far from the homes of the most illustrious men in the colonies, men whose doors were always open to him for his father's sake and Mr. Franklin's, if not his own? Used to the clamor of his large family on the banks of the Schuylkill and his other family on the banks of the Cape Fear, used to making friends like Jane Colden and the McIntoshes and Henry Laurens, he may have felt lonelier at times than other men under similar conditions. And yet no one valued his solitude more than Billy, or sensed its necessity for the kind of life he had chosen—writing, drawing, collecting, and exploring.

There must have been many moments when he longed to live two lives at once, especially at this time when the destiny of the New World was at stake. He may have been contemplating this one day while he prepared to eat his lunch of tongue and cheese and biscuit. He did not have long, though, for contemplation. On looking up, whom should he see approaching but a stout young Cherokee "armed with a rifle gun, and two dogs attending."

"The Cherokees are the largest race of men I ever saw," Billy wrote later. No doubt this young Cherokee appeared to him the largest of them all.

Nevertheless, Billy's gentle smile and extended hand proved disarming. The despised white man then offered tobacco, upon which the Indian, accepting it, "again shook hands and parted in friendship; he descended the hills, singing as he went."

After that, Billy must have felt more confident about his inevitable meeting with Ata-kullakulla, chief of the Cherokees, called at various times White Owl, Leaning Wood, and Little Carpenter.

The exact date of Ata-kullakulla's birth is another of the Smokies' mist-shrouded facts, but some have guessed that it was the same year as John Bartram's. At that time the Cherokees still lived basically in a Stone Age manner, hunting with bows and arrows, spears, and darts. But the white man's gun had recently been introduced to them, and the Indians had become fighters as well as hunters. During the Yamassee War of 1715, English plantation owners were forced to flee to the safety of Charleston and its harbor, where ships were waiting.

But Ata-kullakulla saw the advantages for his people of trade with the British and therefore the necessity of making and maintaining peace with them. As a young man barely thirty, he sailed to England to meet the King. There, decked out in paint and feathers, the White Owl, as he was known then, delighted the British as much by his gestures of friendliness as by his exotic appearance. He had the diplomacy to compare His Majesty, George II, with that ruler of all the universe, the Sun. Hogarth portrayed the Owl, rather ludicrously, in full court regalia; and lords and ladies entertained him.

There is no question that Ata-kullakulla was an unusually civilized and farsighted Indian, and his opportunity to travel enhanced his sophistication. He was naturally anxious that his people enjoy something of what he had known. Flint- and stonework abruptly ceased. Wild animals were dangerously overhunted for the furs so desired in Europe; the money they brought was spent on guns and liquor. "The white people have dazzled their senses with foreign superfluities," wrote Billy sadly.

Still, it had been his loyalty to the English, born from his desire for their trade, that had led the Little Carpenter to spare the life of Captain John Stuart, to whom he vowed lasting friendship and gave the name of "eldest brother."

In 1761, the year after the massacre at Fort Loudon, the Cherokees were finally defeated, and two years later came the end of the French and Indian War. White settlers poured into the fruitful valleys, sometimes called "coves," of the Great Smokies, driving the native inhabitants back into the inhospitable hills. It was hardly any wonder that the Cherokees mistrusted them. But Ata-kullakulla had not forgotten his vow of friendship.

The place where "poor Billy" and the Little Carpenter met has been translated variously as the "top of the world" and the "land of the noonday sun." Billy thought of it as the rooftop of America. Across that rooftop, even though at a distance, Billy observed on the trail ahead an Indian caravan approaching. Riding before it was the chief of the Cherokees. Always small of stature, he appeared at the age of seventy-five exceedingly delicate. Still, he wore his silver jewelry and bore himself with a regal air.

Billy, surmising at once who he was, turned off the path with a gesture of deference and respect, "which compliment was accepted and gratefully and magnanimously returned, for his highness with a gracious and cheerful smile came up to me, and clapping his hand on his breast, offered it to me, saying, I am Ata-cul-culla, and heartily shook hands with me."

There on the path, Billy spoke as easily and confidently to this "wily savage," as some Charlestonians still called him with good reason, as he might have to visitors in his father's garden. He assured him that he had come in peace from Pennsylvania, where his Quaker compatriots felt united in love and brotherhood with the Cherokees, even though dwelling at such a distance apart.

Ata-kullakulla then asked if by chance he knew his old friend John Stuart, whom he was even now on his way to counsel with once more. And eagerly Billy replied that he "had had the honour of a personal acquaintance with the superintendent, the beloved man, who I saw well but the day before I set off and who, by letters to the principal white men in the nation, recommended me to the friendship and protection of the Cherokees."

"To which," Billy went on in his journal, "the great chief was pleased to answer very respectfully, that I was welcome in their country as a friend and brother; and then shaking hands heartily bid me farewell, and his retinue confirmed it by an united voice of assent."

It must have been a remarkable moment, there on the narrow pass beyond the Nantahala River, with Indians, so dangerous that even their beloved superintendent refused Billy the encouragement he sought to visit them, expressing with one voice their brotherhood and trust.

For Billy it was a turning point. He "suddenly came to a resolution" to continue no farther into the over-hill settlements but to return instead to Georgia, and from there set off to Mobile in the West Florida territory. Whether he felt he dared not risk further penetration into the Cherokee Nation, with the chief, an avowed ally, away, or whether he felt that he had already proved his point of friendship was never made clear in Billy's records.

As for Ata-kullakulla, he reached Charleston in time to hear that only days before, Stuart had been forced by the Revolutionaries to flee to Florida because of his Loyalist activities. From there, "Bushyhead" returned to England, where he died at seventy-nine, one year before his Indian "brother," whose age, so far as can be told, was the same as Stuart's.

There can be no doubt that during his long ride back to the white man's civilization the Indians were much in Billy's mind. He had come into the Cherokee Nation to prove something to himself as well as to others.

Brought up with his father's fear and hatred of the Indian, which Mary's horrifying story had partially explained, having heard the traders' and agents' reports of them at Mr. Spalding's Upper and Lower Stores on the San Juan, and having only recently been denied sanction for his visit to the Cherokees by their own superintendent, Billy was perhaps more eager than he otherwise might have been to prove to himself and his world the worth of his redskinned brothers.

"O divine simplicity and truth," Billy wrote of them in his most idealistic mood, "friendship without fallacy or guile, hospitality disinterested, naivete undefiled, unmodified by artificial refinements."

What the young idealist had difficulty in understanding was that the same Cherokee who, because of Billy's obvious desire to please, offered for his horse a supper of corn "which last instance of respect is conferred on those only to whom they manifest the highest esteem, saying that corn was given by the Great Spirit only for food to man," was the very Cherokee who waged a bloody war against the colonists.

This was typical of Billy's sanguine attitude. At the Lower Trading Post, Billy had met the chief of the Seminoles, Mico Chlucco, the Long Warrior.

Mico was the Seminole word for "king"; *Chlucco* meant "excellent"; and the sound of his name was "terrible to his enemies." He was, in fact, that same day on his way to fight the Choctaws. Yet when Puc-Puggy, "the plant hunter," as he called Billy, was in trouble for having killed a rattlesnake in the Seminole camp and thus inciting the snake's descendants to do the Indians harm, the "terrible" Long Warrior intervened and pushed the menacing braves away, "when instantly they altered their countenance and behaviour; they all whooped in chorus . . . and went off, shouting and proclaiming Puc-Puggy was their friend &c."

"Joy seems inherent in them," Billy wrote later, describing what he called "the most striking picture of happiness in this life." They had "nothing to give them disquietude but the gradual encroachments of the white people."

One senses, as well as the prophecy, the innocence and idealism in this account. Billy did not forget this gratitude to Mico Chlucco. Years later, he used the drawing that he had made of him as the frontispiece for his *Travels.*

So it was with Billy and the Indians. And so too, eventually, his reports crossed an ocean and influenced a whole hemisphere of men, who might never see an Indian, to believe that the savage was indeed noble.

It is impossible not to wonder what Dr. John Fothergill, who must have rivaled his old friend Peter Collinson in the qualities of tolerance and patience, thought of this aspect of Billy's report of his expedition, an excursion which, after all, Dr. Fothergill was sponsoring. We may assume that the doctor's concern with the American Indian was negligible compared to his botanical interests.

Puc-Puggy was not, however, so independent and irresponsible as to fail to send, when possible and convenient, specimens and drawings that now, because of growing tensions and hostilities, made their journey under increasing difficulties.

Dr. Fothergill was delighted with Billy's detailed and enthusiastic descriptions, however infrequent, with the unusual plant samples he packed and shipped according to instructions, and particularly with his superb drawings. He sent his protégé praise and encouragement, and, even better, further funds. Billy suddenly saw the chance of making one more dream come true.

Might it not be that still another river, the one the Indians called "Father of Waters," was within his reach? Already he felt that his life, which he had sensed as a sort of river, was marked and bounded by running streams. If he could but glimpse the great Mississippi, sliding between its broad banks, it would be for him a sort of culmination.

Thus it was that the same summer begun in the Appalachians found him as far as Mobile on the Gulf of Mexico, on his way west. By this time it is logical to suppose that the sound of the Massachusetts farmers' shot had reached his ears, even tuned as they had been to little else but birdsong and aboriginal chants.

But Billy had another problem, more immediate and distressing. For longer than he could have expected, considering the delicate health of his boyhood, he had been free from the fevers which had plagued his youth. Since leaving his dank sandbar hermitage near Picolata, he had, in high and airy places, felt remarkably well.

Now, however, near Mobile, he found himself "very ill, and not a little alarmed by an excessive pain in my head, attended with a high fever, this disorder soon settled in my eyes . . . I was incapable of making any observations, for my eyes could not bear the light."

There has been considerable discussion among physicians and others concerning the nature of this illness; diagnoses range from a severe reaction to poison ivy to malaria and scarlet fever.

In any case, he remained seriously ill for a month, fortunately under the constant care of worried strangers who, like others, soon became friends. At last, one morning he awoke "intirely relieved from pain, my senses in perfect harmony and mind composed . . . all was peace and tranquility . . . yet my body seemed but as a light shadow, and my existence as a pleasing delirium, for I sometimes doubted of its reality."

His eyes, though, must have become permanently damaged; as long as fifteen years afterwards, home again on the

Schuylkill, he once more experienced weakness of sight combined with severe eye pain, and he excused himself from correspondence by explaining that he often had to write with his eyes closed.

But Billy would not be deterred from achieving his final dream and, arduous miles later, found he had arrived one evening at Manchac, "where I directed my steps to the banks of the Mississippi, where I stood for a time as it were fascinated by the magnificence of the great sire of rivers."

Nothing in this fulfillment disappointed him. He wrote, "It is not expansion of surface alone that strikes us with ideas of magnificence, the altitude, the theatrical ascents of its pensile banks, the steady course of the mighty flood, the trees, high forests, even every particular object, as well as societies, bear the stamp of superiority and excellence; all unite or combine in exhibiting a prospect of the grand sublime."

His month-long illness and the accompanying pain and frustration of near-blindness had not dimmed his innate enthusiasm, joy, and wonder in what he saw. Nothing in his essentially appreciative and responsive nature had changed.

Naturally he was chafing to get out upon and be a part of that wide stream. And it was not long before he set off with a companion "in a neat Cypress boat with three oars, proceeding up the river."

Here and there, at fine plantations on the water's edge, Billy was entertained by prosperous Frenchmen. "The French here are able, ingenious and industrious planters," he wrote in his journal. "They live easy and plentifully, and are far more regular and commendable in the enjoyment of their earnings than their neighbours the English; their dress of their own manufactures, well wrought and neatly made up, yet not extravagant or foppish; manners and conversation easy, moral and entertaining."

Even while hunting for plant specimens for his father and Dr. Fothergill, Billy found time to be interested in the people and social life around him. Possibly his previous and protracted loneliness had made him more aware of the delights of human companionship.

But it continued to be exploration that mostly occupied his time and mind. In a swamp near the river, he came upon a kind of rotted fossil forest. The dark, rocklike stumps and logs must have reminded him of those that Mary had once shown him, protruding so strangely from the sandy banks of the Cape Fear.

Near the settlement of Baton Rouge he found "an arborescent aromatic vine, which mounts to the tops of the highest trees, by twisting or writhing spirally around them . . . I am entirely ignorant to what genus it belongs." Thirty-five years later, William Bartram was still thinking of his mysterious vine, which he now called *Anonimos,* or "nameless." Botanists have searched for it sporadically ever since.

Billy's days of adventure on the Father of Waters were drawing to an unexpected end. With no apparent warning, his eye infection returned. Typically, he reacted philosophically. "This disappointment affects me very sensibly, but resignation and reason resuming their empire over my mind, I submitted and determined to return to Carolina."

January of 1776 found him in Georgia, near the Ocmulgee, "in view of the foaming flood of the river, now raging over its banks." As he camped there on a warm and calm evening, a woodcock was singing its flight song overhead, uttering a melodic series of notes while soaring high in the air, and then plummeting to earth and calling plaintively for a mate.

Billy heard the courtship song in a mood of unusual dejec-

tion. That afternoon some traders from Augusta had joined
his party, and it is probable that they brought fresh news of
the progress of the Rebellion. As a Quaker, Billy had professed himself "against War & violence, in any form or
manner whatever." Now, though, his country was committed
to a struggle for the independence its leaders felt it must
have, a struggle which it appeared to be in grave danger of
losing.

Needing to be alone for cogitation, Billy had wandered
that evening into "the expansive fields, fragrant groves and
sublime forests" that he had always delighted in and from
which more than once he had sought solace. There is little
doubt that he was asking himself, and perhaps his God, what
he should do. In his concern for his native land, he may even
have thought of himself as strong and well, overlooking the
recurrent fevers that had caused him to abandon adventures
and exploration.

Whether he reached any conclusion in this solitary roaming and soul-searching he did not record, but on returning to
his companions he found them "cheerful and thoughtless
rather to an extreme." That summer he volunteered to join
General Lachlan McIntosh's military detachment in Georgia.

Billy had first met the McIntosh family on a spring day in
1773, almost at the outset of his travels. Three years later,
when he returned to Georgia on his way to Carolina, he did
not fail to stop again at the house near the banks of the
Altamaha. There he found much changed. Lachlan, twelve
or fourteen years older than Billy, was now an officer in
charge of a battalion of Georgians. The British had come as
far south as Savannah and had attacked Charleston. There
was talk of an invasion of Georgia from a British base at St.
Augustine. So Billy, with scenes from other years poignantly
in his mind, and with anxiety for friends and places, set aside
his Quaker professions and offered to Lachlan McIntosh and
to his country his services as a soldier.

One can only be thankful that the deeply concerned young man, so torn in his convictions and still unsure of his health, was not forced to engage in combat and killing. The rumored invasion did not occur after all; the detachment disbanded, and Billy turned to the pleasant and peaceable task of finding his father's long-lost mystery tree.

It has been suggested, although there seem to be no definite records of this, that while Billy was ostensibly occupied with plant-hunting that summer of 1776, he was actually also secretly scouting for Lachlan McIntosh. Since the disbanding of the Georgia detachment, the explorer may have been doing intelligence reconnoitering for his friend. Unarmed, and quite obviously a botanist engaged in collecting and sketching, he would, if encountered, certainly have seemed innocent enough and hardly a cause for suspicion.

One evening, while traveling alone through a glade of fragrant pines, he was startled to glimpse a Seminole armed with a rifle, crossing his path a little distance ahead. Billy's first impulse was to hide. Slipping behind a tree trunk, he waited in a state of agitation, but it was too late; the Indian had seen him and was galloping forward, gun at the ready, "his countenance angry and fierce."

Billy, unarmed, knew that he was at his mercy. Thoughts of his father and grandfather swarmed in his mind. He resigned himself to the Seminole's will and to that of the Almighty. Then he went forward and held out his hand.

This was obviously the last thing the Indian had expected. His glare of malice, rage, and disdain dissolved into disconcertion, and finally, "with dignity in his look and action," he took Billy's hand. There in the wilderness two ancient enemies shared a moment of friendship. His expression, Billy related that night to the men at the trading house on the banks of the St. Marys River, seemed to say: "Go to thy brethren, tell them thou sawest an Indian in the forests, who knew how to be humane and compassionate."

The group at the trading house also had a story to tell. That Indian was described as "one of the greatest villains on earth, a noted murderer, and outlawed by his countrymen." The evening before, the traders had broken his gun and beaten him with it, but he had stolen a new one, with which he had vowed to kill the first white man he met.

The men marveled at Billy's narrow and miraculous escape, as he did, himself, thanking his Creator that he had been given the confidence to make the disarming gesture of gentleness. And then, as he considered his experience alone and in tranquillity, he began to crystallize his philosophy toward the Indians and all untutored peoples, and even animals, in which he had already sensed a spiritual quality.

Set down on paper years later, his tenet had not changed. "Can it be denied, but that the moral principle, which directs the savages to virtuous and praiseworthy actions, is natural or innate? It is certain they have not the assistance of letters, or those means of education in the schools of philosophy, where the virtuous sentiments and actions of the most illustrious characters are recorded, and carefully laid before the youth of civilized nations: therefore this moral principle must be innate, or they must be under the immediate influence and guidance of a more divine and powerful preceptor, who, on these occasions, instantly inspires them, and as with a ray of divine light, points out to them at once the dignity, propriety, and beauty of virtue."

That same summer, he found his father's tree "in perfect bloom." Five snow-white petals in a corolla surrounded a cluster of bright yellow stamens. The petals were ruffled or "crisped" at the borders and were "ornamented with a crown or tassel of gold-coloured refulgent stamina in their centre." So William Bartram, years later in his study at home, was to describe the bloom of this "very curious tree."

He and his father had been inclined to believe it a species of Gordonia, but upon examination of the fragrant flowers, almost four inches in diameter, which had not been there for him to see before, he "presently found striking characteristics abundantly sufficient to separate it from that genus, and to establish it the head of a new tribe, which we have honoured with the name of the illustrious Dr. Benjamin Franklin, *Franklinia Alatamaha*."

This, though, was published years afterward. In the meantime, a Philadelphia horticulturist and cousin of Billy's, Humphrey Marshall, described in 1785 in his *Arbustrum Americanum* the *Franklinia alatamaha*, using Billy's spelling of the river name, and thus it has remained.

The first edition of Bartram's *Travels* did not come out until six years later, a year after Moses Marshall had gone hunting for the *Franklinia alatamaha* and collected most of those lost trees in the deep woods of Georgia.

It is reasonable to assume that Billy, standing before the tree his father had been so eager for him to rediscover, was not thinking about the publication of books. It is far more likely to imagine that he was dreaming of Kingsessing.

Always a reluctant letter writer, he yearned just the same for news of his family. Earlier he had written to his "Honour'd and Benevolent Father: . . . I am happy by the blessings of the Almighty God by whose care I have been protected & led safe through a Pilgrimage these three & twenty months." He had signed himself "ever your faithful Son" and wistfully added that he had "not had the favour of a line from my Father or Mother whom God ever preserve."

Presumably military activities, of which Billy had but the vaguest notion, prevented deliveries of mail. And there were still hostile Indians on many trails. Some of Billy's friends had already given him up as lost among the savages.

But his father, in spite of his old and deep-seated fear, must have remembered his son's impatience with correspon-

dence and his casual ways that were once called irresponsible. And he also must have recalled his ease of manner and
inborn sense of brotherhood with his fellow man, of whatever color or creed. John, in his late seventies now, and
suffering such dimness of sight that he pleaded with his
friend Ben to send him new lenses, still did not doubt that he
would see his "little botanist" again.

The botanist, who was also an artist, sat that fine summer
day sketching his "beautiful flowering tree," with its finely
striped gray-and-pearl bark, its round nutlike fruit, its slender shining leaves which rose gracefully with an upright,
springing resilience on delicate stems. Twelve years later he
would paint it in what some have called his most valuable
watercolor. The original is in the British Museum, but a
copy hangs in the house John Bartram built on the banks of
the Schuylkill.

Also hanging there is a print by possibly the greatest, and
certainly the most famous, bird artist of all—John James
Audubon. The bird in the print is the rare Bachman's war-
bler, named by Audubon for a friend of his, John Bachman,
the Charleston minister. The reason for the picture's being in
Billy's old home is that the bird is drawn perched on a
blossoming branch of Franklinia, "one of the most beautiful
of our southern flowers," as Audubon wrote of it. He made
his painting in the fall of 1833, exactly sixty-eight years from
the time that the new Botanist to the King and his shop-
keeper son had first stood before the mysterious scarlet
leaves aglow in the sunset.

Billy collected more of its seeds, and it is fortunate that he
did, because he had not found it growing elsewhere in the
southeast wilderness. Nor has it been found anywhere except in cultivation, since very early in the nineteenth century.
For some reason, it disappeared completely from its grove
by the Altamaha.

Belonging to the tea family, a chiefly Asiatic group which

includes Gordonias, Stewartias, and the ornamental camellias, some Franklinias still grow in John Bartram's garden. They have also been planted near Independence Hall and the Liberty Bell in Philadelphia, and as far north as Boston, Benjamin Franklin's birthplace. A few also graced the Royal Gardens at Kew.

In collecting the fruit and drawing the flowers, Billy must have felt that he was fulfilling a dream as important to him as his sight of the Mississippi, because, in a way, it was his father's dream too. He had made this a kind of pilgrimage for both of them. Now he was ready to go home. But before he did, there was one more pilgrimage to make.

Not surprisingly, it was to the Cape Fear. To the place where he had spent many of the happiest and most meaningful days of his life, Billy felt compelled to return once more.

Whether he guessed or knew that it would be his final visit, who can say? He must have felt a certain sense of finality, as well as relief, when the last of his samples set sail for London. He realized that his recovery from his fevers had been slower than he had anticipated, that traveling was more of an effort for him now than it had been, that he felt older than his thirty-seven years.

There is no doubt at all that he was depressed by the war. He had avoided as much as possible discussing it in Charleston, and his friends, aware of his Quaker background, may have respected this and been more circumspect than they ordinarily might have been over their teacups and julep mugs. In any case, his return to Ashwood, his former shelter from the world, was bound to be more distressing than he could have dreamed.

The time in this momentous year of 1776 was December, when customarily preparations for Christmas would have filled the air with excitement. "Oh, Billy, thee is here!" cried Mary Robeson, running down the steps and embracing him. In a moment she was surrounded by her children: Bartram,

Jonathan, William, and Elizabeth. Mary put her hand on William's head. "This is 'my Billy' now. Thee has not met him before."

Two of her other William Bartrams were gone. Her father had died in 1770, and there was already a legend that he had drowned in the lake beside which stood his mill, the lake that bore his name. Her brother, William Jr., the physician, had died less than two years later, treating patients in the yellow-fever epidemic that had also taken his mother's life. A legend sprang up about him too. They said that the ghost of Polly White, who loved the young doctor so much that on his death she cast herself into the Cape Fear River, haunted the halls of Ashwood, walking up and down in a wedding dress she never wore in life.

In the rooms where the family had so often gathered, Mary, for the children's sake, was making an attempt to decorate for Christmas. Garlands of native smilax and mistletoe hung over doors and windows; glossy leaves of magnolia reflected the filtered light from the river; tawny oak leaves, pale stalks of dried wheat, and the red berries of yaupon stood about in Chinese porcelain jars.

With her slender palm, Mary pushed from her brow a strand of hair, already turning gray, Billy noticed. "Had I known when thee was coming, I might have greeted thee in more stylish fashion. But thee is no less welcome. The war has taken both our funds and our desire for fine attire."

Billy remembered to ask for her husband. Mary looked proud. "For two years Tom has been a delegate from the county to the North Carolina Provincial Congress at Halifax, up near the Virginia border. He maintains his hope of returning here for Christmas. I dare not tell the children how slim this hope is. The Rebellion, as thee knows, does not go well for us; we count on nothing now." She paused for a moment, her eyes cast down and sad, and then she turned back to him with her familiar sweet smile. "Thee knows that thee is welcome to pass the holiday with us in thy beloved uncle's home, and also at Walnut Grove. I do not forget our youthful days, my cousin, when we were free of care. Tom would not forgive me were I not to detain thee here until his return."

Touched by her invitation, as well as by her confidence in her husband's safety, Billy was tormented by a desire simply to rest and remain with her and her children during the holidays in that peaceful house on the high bank of the river, with its expansive prospect of cane field and woodland.

But another kind of urge, equally strong, tugged at him to continue on to Kingsessing. "Mary," he murmured so softly and with such regret in his voice that she leaned forward and stared at him anxiously, "I must go home; I have no choice but to continue on my way. My father is an old man now. He may not live to see many more Christmases. And I am led to believe that this war may come close to Philadelphia. Whether I am needed there or not, it is where I should be. I may already have been away too long."

Mary called to her servant Cezar to bring a pitcher of punch and some fruitcake that Old Betty had baked that autumn and stored in a metal chest in the root cellar.

"Cezar and Old Betty are *Robeson* slaves," Billy commented.

"Well, I'm a Robeson now," Mary said simply.

Billy remarked that he would have expected to find Old Cloe and Little Cloe and Lonzo at Ashwood, where they had always been.

"Mother left all to Sarah," said Mary, as simply as before.

"All of her slaves?" Billy asked, astonished.

"All of everything: land, stock, slaves, silver. It is only because my sister married General Brown and has her own plantation now that I am allowed to remain here. Behind the bricks in my father's old kitchen, Tom has concealed the notes from his men for money he advanced to them for supplies for their families while the soldiers were engaged in combat. Sarah and Thomas Brown have been generous and understanding. But as soon as my Tom is able to complete his new house on the upper terrace above the old dwelling at Walnut Grove, we shall move there. His brother, Peter, will be just across the river, and an avenue, one quarter of a mile in length, has already been cut through the trees to the water's edge, so that we may send signals and invitations." To Billy she seemed surprisingly content, far more than he was.

"I can hardly believe it," he said, going back to what was on his mind. "Aunt Elizabeth left thee nothing at all?"

Cezar, thin and dark as gingerbread, came with the punch and a plate of thinly sliced cake. "Thee must try this cake," Mary persuaded Billy. "It has rum from Barbados in it, and who knows when we shall have more? Ah, well—" and she sat on a small footstool beside him—"if that is all that the Rebellion takes from us, we shall be fortunate indeed."

When Cezar had left them, she answered Billy's question. "Ten pounds she left. A token that she had not inadvertently overlooked a daughter named Mary. And even that not to me outright, but to be handed me by Sarah, and then no more. Those were the words in her will; I saw them with these eyes: 'and no more.' I shall never cease wondering why."

Billy turned away from the pain of her bewilderment, and as he did a cloud passed before the sun, casting a shadow into the room. And Billy saw another shadow from years before and heard a voice saying, "I shall punish Mary later in my own way."

"What can I do for thee, my dearest cousin?" Billy asked then, fervently. It was as though he were asking her how he could make it up to her.

But Mary only smiled and protested that she had everything she wanted and lacked or regretted very little. "We have had violence here," she added, "but praise God it is safely past."

Then in ran Bartram, at twelve the eldest of her children; he had his eye on the cake. "It's all right," Mary told him tolerantly. "This is a special occasion and reason for celebration. Only a crumb, though, child; more might cause thee to fall down. We shall have many a fruitcake," she added, patting him fondly, "when we are all living again at Walnut Grove."

After the boy had left the room, Billy asked Mary to what violence she had referred. She looked at him in astonishment. "Why, our battle here, last winter. I cannot believe thee did not hear of it." Then her face softened. "But of course, my phoebe, thee was doubtless flying somewhere through the wilderness miles away."

Billy blushed. "Out of some sort of consideration, I suppose, my acquaintances have told me little. No report of any encounter here has reached my ears."

And so, while her cousin raptly listened, Mary told him of the battle that has been called "The Lexington and Concord of the South." The Loyalist Scottish Highlanders, many of them only recently moved to the New World and naturally reluctant to go to war with the mother country, had come to Cross Creek for a gathering of the clan. They had been summoned by the Royal Governor of North Carolina, Josiah Martin, who had succeeded William Tryon.

To assuage his young wife in her sorrow over the death of their son, Tryon had spent four years planning and supervising the construction of a "palace," in New Bern on the Neuse River, that has been called "the most beautiful building in the Colonial Americas." Ironically, Tryon resided there only a few months before he was summoned away to become governor of New York.

The Loyalist Highlanders had received an optimistic message from Governor Martin that Sir Henry Clinton and Lord

Cornwallis would arrive with the full support of an expeditionary force, prepared for an invasion of North Carolina and engagements with the Whig patriots. The June before, those same Whigs had pledged to "go forth and be ready to sacrifice our lives and fortunes to secure freedom and safety."

The Highlanders, many in their kilts, marched that winter of 1776 along the South River and the Black River Road from Cross Creek, on their way to Wilmington and to Clinton and Cornwallis. They never reached their destination.

Following the winding course of the Cape Fear River, the patriots, led by Colonel James Moore of the First North Carolina Regiment, cut off the Tories at the only crossing of a fifty-foot-wide swampy stream. Colonel Moore knew about the bridge because it spanned his own property.

There, in the bitter cold of the February night, the Whigs removed the planks from the floor of the bridge, greased the girders, and waited behind concealed earthworks for the Highlanders to try to cross. It was a complete rout. Whatever Tories were able to make their way across the demolished bridge were annihilated by Whig gunfire. The rest fled in total retreat.

Colonel Moore reported to a member of the Provincial Council: "Thus, sir, I have the pleasure to inform you, has most happily terminated a very dangerous insurrection and will, I trust, put an effectual check to Toryism in this country." It did more than check the Tories, and it did more than prevent the British invasion; it inspired North Carolina to be the first colony to vote in favor of independence at the Continental Congress.

"Thee can imagine the pride and excitement here," Mary went on. "But oh, Billy, this is a hard time to be a Quaker." Dusk had fallen in the paneled room, made even darker by the wreaths at the windows. Only the familiar pale light from the river lit the ceiling; Mary had made no move to seek tapers.

"So our bridge is gone," Billy said at last.

Mary put her lips against his fingers. "We were two children in another world," she whispered. "It is well we did not know what lay ahead."

She drew away then. "Anyway, Billy, the bridge is famous now. In London they scoff at it and say that a battle with a name like "Moore's Creek Bridge" could hardly have extensive consequences. Thus they attempt to laugh away their loss. Yet at the council our representatives report that the skirmish has changed our rebellion into a revolution."

She went then for some candles, and when she returned, Billy was calling to Bartram to fetch his horse. Once more Mary urged him to stay. "Thee cannot arrive at Kingsessing by Christmastime, however swiftly thee travels. The ground in the north is hard and frozen now, and the days are at their shortest. Worse than that, armed scouts and enemies lurk everywhere."

Still, Billy would not be persuaded. He kissed his cousin without saying what was in his mind, that he might never see her again. And he shook hands with little William, his namesake, with the same sense of finality. How could he have known that by the time he died, a famous and revered old man with many honors, little William's own son would be the age of Bartram, who now brought his horse?

Mary's prophecy proved correct; Christmas found Billy only as far north as Virginia. In Maryland he was confronted with unfamiliar drifts, "now deep everywhere around, the air cold to an extreme, and the roads deep under snow or slippery with ice."

Cautiously crossing the Susquehanna, "examining well our icy bridge, and being careful of our steps, we landed safe on the opposite shore . . . and in two days more arrived at my father's house on the banks of the river Schuylkill."

John Bartram's "little botanist" had come home.

CHAPTER 7

HOME TO THE RIVER

"Knowing that Nature never did betray
The heart that loved her."

William Wordsworth

The river was jammed with ice. Billy, standing on its bank beside his father's old cider press, could not remember in all his forty-three years seeing the stream so completely free of traffic. No boats of any kind departed from Gray's Ferry. The only movement passing before his eyes was made by broken chunks of ice, joggling each other and weaving down the clogged current. Otherwise the frozen landscape held no activity at all; everything seemed hung in balance and waiting, except where overhead a flock of chickadees fluttered and wheezed in the buckeye branches.

The year was 1783 and only two days old.

Billy's thoughts strayed from the scene confronting him to the day before, when he had entertained a distinguished visitor. He had heard that Thomas Jefferson was in the city. Jefferson's frigate, the *Romulus*, which was to have carried him to France to conclude the signing of the peace treaty, had been blocked up in the ice of Baltimore harbor, with no foreseeable prospect of liberation. Never one to waste time, Jefferson had proceeded overland to Philadelphia to study pertinent papers in the office of state. But on New Year's Day he had paid a surprise visit to Kingsessing.

Nancy Bartram, the daughter of Billy's younger brother, John, to whom the house and garden now belonged, had welcomed the handsome tawny-haired stranger, but it was Billy whom he requested to see. He hastened to express his condolences to Bartram upon the death of his esteemed and remarkable father. Jefferson had had the news from Henry Laurens, now in Paris with Benjamin Franklin, preparing the preliminaries of peace.

Beside Dr. Franklin's stove in the deep-walled room, whose windows, hand-carved by the elder Bartram, looked out on the snowy afternoon, and near the fireplace cupboards where John had dried his seeds before sending them across the ocean, the two friends sipped his famous cider.

Tom Jefferson, already noted for his discriminating taste in food and drink, remarked that he was happy to see the receipt for the cider had not changed. He was, he admitted, not partial to the more ardent spirits, such as the popular rum punch concocted at the State in Schuylkill Club. In his home at Monticello he prepared a spiced cider with a few sticks of cinnamon and a handful of whole cloves. He would, he said at once, be most happy if Mr. Bartram would honor him with a visit at the first convenient occasion, not merely to sample his wine cellar, which also contained persimmon beer, but to offer as well advice upon his garden. Fruits and vegetables, he added, he had always valued above any kind of meat.

Young Jefferson's Virginia mountaintop garden was well known. It was reported that he was exceedingly fastidious about his plantings, keeping careful records of his crops, always attentive to new and hardier strains, and predicting with astonishing accuracy the dates when the first peas and lettuces would appear on his table.

Billy would give much to be able to walk on those serpentine brick paths, past the espaliered trees, into the scientifically ordered flower beds. But he sensed that his days of travel were at an end, and he had said as much to his friend.

Jefferson had looked up with a quizzical frown. Billy was, after all, but a few scant years his senior, and Tom's travels seemed just to be commencing. How, he wondered, could his companion contemplate abandoning his journeying when so much of the undiscovered world awaited?

It had long been his dream, Jefferson confided to his host, to explore the land that lay beyond the great flood of the Mississippi. And yet he realized that he often expressed the conflicting wish to remain at home in his garden. Politics, he felt, destroys happiness; yet here he was deeply enmeshed in his country's future.

His hazel eyes had darkened as he stared through the uncurtained windows to where bands of clouds, rolling in from the west, looked as though at any moment they would deposit more snow. Until winter relented, he would progress no farther than this eastern coast, where, up and down the shore, the waiting ships lay trapped in ice.

Billy was thinking of his friend's dream of the Mississippi. He himself, alas, had been seriously ill there. Indeed, he had still not recovered. Only the past summer he had been forced, because of uncertain health, to decline an invitation from the University of the State of Pennsylvania to serve as Professor of Botany. He mentioned this to Tom. Jefferson said that it had been a great loss to the university.

Billy inquired then as to the health of their friend Henry Laurens, and Jefferson replied that he feared Laurens was far from well. His imprisonment in the Tower had taken its toll upon his body, and his spirit might never recover from the death of his son, who had survived all of General Washington's battles from Brandywine to Yorktown, only to be killed in a minor skirmish afterward.

Jefferson wondered whether the close approach of Burgoyne's army at Brandywine in that September of 1777 had precipitated John Bartram's sudden death.

So Billy told him that all during the bitterly cold journey from North Carolina, as 1776 turned into 1777, his constant fear had been that he would not return to Kingsessing in time to find his father alive. But the Creator, as always, had been kind. John, in reasonably good health, had welcomed him back. They had had, Billy ventured to assure Jefferson, a most tender reunion.

Yet there was no question, he admitted, that the magnitude of his father's anxiety for his family and his home, with the British encamped so near, had hastened his death. His doctors agreed. But there was something else that Billy wanted to say.

His friend Tom had recently suffered a far more serious loss. His wife, the lovely Martha Skelton, was dead. Hardly knowing how to choose his words, Billy offered his inadequate consolation.

The young statesman from Virginia stretched his long legs toward the stove and looked into the coals. That day, he said, the beginning of the new year, would have marked their eleventh wedding anniversary. It was the first that he had spent alone. He had sought solace in John Bartram's house, he explained, because it had never failed to offer him serenity.

To his horror, Billy felt his eyes burn with tears. There was no hiding this awkward phenomenon from his observant companion, even though he turned his glance to the bare terraces and leafless trees, upon which snow, in flakes as large as pigeon feathers, was finally starting to fall. He begged Tom to forgive his unmanly weakness. His father and his cousin Mary Robeson, among others, had chided him for his sentimentality; he was mortified that he had not yet learned to control it.

Jefferson's expression seemed to borrow softness from the snow-laden air. He spoke of how he had always valued sensitivity and concern for others. And then, rising to leave, he praised Colonel Thomas Robeson. He remembered that the hero of the Cape Fear, and indeed of all Carolina and the southern colonies, was married to Billy's cousin. He sometimes thought, he added whimsically, that were he not Tom Jefferson, he would most prefer to be Tom Robeson.

With all this in mind, Billy turned from the river, where he had been watching the ice floes, and made his way up the white-etched path. The snow had ceased; a band of sunset light glowed between purple clouds on the western horizon. The morning would doubtless dawn cold and clear, with a sky like blue porcelain. Billy trudged along, thinking of Jefferson's last words and of Colonel Robeson, the hero and Mary's husband.

How could they have dreamed, Billy and his beloved cousin, when they rode as children through the woods and fields along the river, that one day their countryside would be historic ground and that young Tom of Walnut Grove would emerge in a kind of glory; that Tom and his brother, Peter, would come to be called the "Hotspurs of the Cape Fear"?

Just as their bridge, where Colonel Moore's creek ran underneath, had become familiar from Philadelphia to London, so the deep, vine-draped ravine at Bladen Court House that they had delighted in exploring was destined to be known far and wide as the "Tory Hole." There, on a moonlit summer night in 1781, a small band of patriots whom Tom had volunteered to lead drove to its doom an astonished and suddenly retreating foe, many of them His Majesty's Loyalist subjects, the Scottish Highlanders.

During the years after the battle of Moore's Creek Bridge, the Cape Fear valley had been a relatively peaceful place. Vegetables flourished in the fertile meadows and were sent to General Washington's army. Flax turned golden in the autumn sun and was spun into cloth for uniforms. Cattle and pigs were raised and driven to northern markets. Carolina soldiers, who had rarely seen snow, made their way to Valley Forge.

Elizabethtown, the seat of prosperous Bladen County, had been named in 1773, the story went, for the sweetheart of a man called Isaac Jones, who had given the land on the west bank of the river for a town site. Ships passed daily on their way between Cross Creek and the Frying Pan Shoal. In the chilly spring of 1781, General Cornwallis marched from Cross Creek to Wilmington on a journey that was to lead eventually to Yorktown. Tories along the way looked out from their windows and cheered. Some may even have assumed the rebellion was over.

But the Whigs were taking nothing for granted. And had they not been victorious at Elizabethtown, they might well have been entirely wiped out of the valley. So it was reported later.

Tom and his little group, far outnumbered by the enemy, who had captured and pillaged their homes, ventured everything on one last effort. Creeping up the opposite side of the river, and wading or swimming across, with musket and bayonet they surprised the invaders where they camped at the river's edge. Dawn had not yet broken; the Loyalists lay sleeping. Half dreaming, they heard the watchword "Washington" pass from Whig to Whig and were convinced that General Washington himself had come to rout them. Their first thought was to run for their lives. Most of them tumbled into a bushy gully, the V-shaped wedge of which pointed from the river into the main street of the town. Some accidentally plunged headlong into the gorge; some purposely sought shelter there. Very few emerged.

Tory power along the Cape Fear River was broken; it was never a threat again. And it had been Tom Robeson, without so much as a commission at the time, who had accomplished this. So Mary's cousin mused on.

Billy's niece Ann, or Nancy as he called her, was awaiting him, thawing out water in the stone trough. "Uncle Billy," she cried, "was not thy visitor yesterday that same Mr. Jefferson who wrote our Declaration? I was the one to open the door when he stood without, so pretty with his russet hair and olive eyes. Is he important?"

Billy enjoyed teasing her. "God made him; therefore he must be important."

Ann loved her uncle as much as he loved her. "Thee knows full well that is not what I meant. God made us all, even old Tom, thy crow, but *we* are not important. I mean, is he important like Grandfather, or Dr. Franklin, or General Washington?"

"Ah," said Billy, "thee means, will he live on in the history books; will he be famous? Well, Nancy, Mr. Jefferson has acknowledged on several occasions that what he really desires is to remain at his home in Virginia and tend his garden, in which he takes much pride. Now that he is a widower with two young daughters to care for, he may well decide to do exactly that. If so, I pray it makes him content, but it is not likely to make him famous."

It was eight years later, in 1791, that the *Travels* of William Bartram, which were certainly to make Billy famous, were published by James and Johnson in Philadelphia. The complete title was: "Travels through North & South Carolina, Georgia, East & West Florida, the Cherokee Country, the Extensive Territories of the Muscogulges, or Creek Confederacy, and the Country of the Chactaws; containing An Account of the Soil and Natural Productions of those Regions, Together with Observations on the Manners of the Indians." The work was "embellished with copper-plates," the frontispiece being Billy's drawing of Mico Chlucco, the Long Warrior, chief of the Seminoles.

Subscriptions to Billy's account of his journeys had been issued as early as five years before. Tom Jefferson had been one of the first to subscribe. At that time, Billy had proposed to dedicate the volume to Benjamin Franklin. A mutual friend had written to Franklin that "Mr. Bartram wishes that it might be dedicated to you as his father had the pleasure of being acquainted with you and professed the highest esteem."

In the April of the year before the book was published, however, Dr. Franklin, then eighty-four, ill and in pain, remarked that "a dying man can do nothing easy," and breathed his last. Regretfully, Billy was forced to reconsider his dedication. With some trepidation, due largely to his innate abhorrence of war, he approached General Washington, now also known as the "Father of his Country."

The President, though, felt forced to decline the dedication, explaining that he had refused "several similar applications" and did not wish to give offense by accepting this one. Since Washington had made several trips to John Bartram's garden to sit under his favorite buckeye tree and in the leafy arbor that was known as "Washington's," one may assume that he declined the proffered dedication with considerable regret. Like Jefferson, he had been known to claim that he preferred planting to politics, and like Jefferson he had also been an early subscriber to the *Travels*.

The honor of dedication finally fell upon Major General Thomas Mifflin, another military man although a birthright Friend, and the first governor of Pennsylvania.

"This volume of Travels is gratefully inscribed by his respectful friend and servant William Bartram," wrote Billy, thereby bestowing upon the new governor an unexpected form of immortality.

The *Travels* was published in London the following year. Dr. Fothergill, the man who more than anyone except its author had made the book possible, had died on Boxing Day in 1780, twelve years before. But Peter Collinson's son Michael was alive.

After his father's death, Michael had kept in touch with John, whom he had never seen but with whom he felt he had much in common. Like the Bartrams, Michael believed that every animal contained "a heavenly spark, derived from the Great Author and Fountain of Life."

But Michael was baffled and hurt by the colonists' rejection of the mother country. In particular, he could not understand John's patriotic attitude, when he had been named, after all, Botanist to the King and provided with a royal pension. "It is a disagreeable subject and we will, if you please, drop it," he wrote in his last letter to his father's friend. Just the same, it is highly probable that he read Billy's book with more than passing interest.

The spirit of John Bartram is everywhere in the *Travels*. His wisdom, enthusiasm, encouragement, and faith shine through the pages like a guiding star. Close to the end of the book, Billy paid specific tribute to his father as "the American botanist and traveller, who contributed as much if not more than any other man towards enriching the North American botanical nomenclature, as well as its natural history."

In 1794 a second edition was published in London. A young poet named Coleridge happened upon it and was enthralled. "The latest book of travels I know written in the spirit of the old travellers," he said, "is Bartram's account of his tour in the Floridas. It is a work of high merit in every way."

That same year, the *Travels* came out in Holland. The year before, it had been published in Dublin and Berlin. In France, two editions were sold. On both sides of the ocean, it was acclaimed. Great men of many nations flocked to the garden on the banks of the Schuylkill. It would seem that Billy had an undreamed-of and ultimate glory. But more was to come.

It came early in the new century. Nancy Bartram burst into his study. "Uncle Billy!" she squeaked. "The President of our land is waiting upon thee."

Billy Bartram had seen Tom Jefferson several times during the summer of 1793 when Jefferson, then Secretary of State, and seeking to escape the yellow-fever epidemic threatening Philadelphia, had taken a house "in the country," as he wrote, at Gray's Ferry for the summer. But now was the first time that the two men had met since the President had moved the capital to Washington.

They sat in the arbor in which John Bartram and Ben Franklin had once sought the shade, and which George Washington had called his own, and they looked out onto the broad river. Ships moved freely now, and between them and the pale marshes of the Delaware, farmhouses and barns had sprung up on the meadows of the Schuylkill. "You may have moved our capital, but not our population," Billy observed.

Jefferson remarked with admiration that Philadelphia was still the most cultivated city in the land, being both the artistic and social center. And he suggested that Mr. Peale's museum, in addition to the Philosophical Society, made it the scientific center as well.

Charles Willson Peale, the Maryland-born artist who had

already painted several portraits of General Washington and would in 1808 paint William Bartram, had another and more unusual interest—that of shooting birds and mammals and mounting them for exhibit. He later became one of America's first recognized taxidermists.

Peale's unique hobby led to his establishing a natural-history museum, to which both Jefferson and Franklin, as well as many others, contributed. Natural history as a science was attracting more and more students. To encourage them, the remarkable Peale had arranged his mounted animals in realistic settings with suitable dried vegetation, "artificial rocks," and appropriate scenic backgrounds, some of them painted by his artistic, and artistically named, sons. The now-familiar habitat group display was thus originated in Willson Peale's museum.

It was a fine spring day. Bluebirds sang softly in Lady Petre's pear tree, which was in full, fragrant bloom. John Bartram had written of the tree to Collinson, "I think a better is not in the world."

A pair of flycatchers flew about, adding twigs and mud to an old nest in the eaves of the seed house. Jefferson watched them with interest and wondered aloud whether the same birds returned year after year, and if so, how they managed to find their way.

Billy remembered that, as a boy of fourteen making his first drawings, he had pondered the same thing. He still had no answer, but he had been keeping records of the dates on which the "birds of passage" arrived in the spring. The kingfisher had come early this year; the phoebes were tardy. So far, he had found no way of making certain that they were the identical birds of previous years. If only there were some way of marking them . . . But it was a fantastic idea.

Birds were perhaps the most elusive of all creatures, timorous, unapproachable, always on the wing.

Thinking of phoebes, he mentioned to his guest that Colonel Robeson's widow had departed this life late in the last century.

Mary, after Tom's death in 1785, had married a Colonel James Morehead, also a Whig hero of the Carolinas, but Billy continued to think of her as Mary Robeson. While she was still a widow, he had written assuring her that time could never "erace from my mind those impressions which it received during my residence in my Unkles family in No. Carolina; Dreams by Night, or serious reveres by day, often present to my emagination striking senes of past transactions, which occur'd to me in your delightful country; & be assured that thou [here 'you' had been written, crossed out, and 'thou' substituted] my Cousen [first a small 'c', then shaped into a large one] art the formost pleasing Object in these Ideal paintings."

After expressing his sympathy, Jefferson somewhat obliquely commented upon the fact that Billy had never married. He quickly put aside his friend's mild protest by complaining that he himself had been under considerable pressure from his acquaintances to remarry and provide a new mother for his daughters and particularly a hostess for the President's House. Nothing, he maintained, could be more distasteful to him. One did not love as he had loved Martha Skelton, and then love another. He was sure that Billy understood.

Actually, he went on still rather obscurely, the fact that Mr. Bartram had no direct dependents might serve them both well. Not until then did he indicate that he had come to Kingsessing on an urgent and significant mission. He prayed that Mr. Bartram would bestow upon him his full attention —he had seen Billy's glance straying to the tall trees—and that he would grant the request he had come that day to make.

Billy squinted at his friend quizzically. Since he had undertaken the burdens of his high office, Tom's chestnut hair had become shot here and there with gray, giving it a sandy look. His high nose, with its wide nostrils, was a trifle thinner, his strong chin more jutting; but his tawny-green eyes were, if possible, keener than ever, and now they took on a glow that appeared to come from within.

He seemed to be looking off beyond the Delaware to the Mississippi, and even farther. When he began to speak, he mentioned distant and vaguely defined western boundaries. He felt strongly the necessity, as well as the responsibility, of having purchased from Bonaparte that largely unexplored land known as the Louisiana Territory.

Bartram had naturally heard of this transaction and had been instantly impressed by Jefferson's farsightedness, although he was aware that many disagreed with him and considered that little had been bought but the paper the title was printed on. He was quick to congratulate his friend on his negotiation. Napoleon himself had admitted that this accession of territory affirmed forever the power of the United States, adding that he had "just given England a maritime rival that sooner or later will lay low her pride."

Warmly, Billy told his friend that he had performed an invaluable service for his country.

Tom seemed particularly pleased by this response. He had been criticized from many sources for what was felt to be a rash, inconsequent, and even unconstitutional act. Always sensitive, he was eager now to justify to all Americans what Talleyrand had already termed a "noble bargain." It was essential, therefore, to ascertain what the new acquisition consisted of: its boundaries, its resources, and its economic and military advantages. In short, he must prove its value and determine the land's best usage.

He then turned upon Billy a fiery look. He was, he said, proposing an expedition of exploration. He had a private secretary from his own home county, a Captain Meriwether Lewis, who had agreed to lead the venture. Another officer and Virginian, George Rogers Clark's younger brother, William, would assist him in conducting a detachment of possibly thirty soldiers and a third as many civilians.

He waited a moment, his eyes still full of fire, and then added that he would not be Tom Jefferson if he did not yearn to be a member of the party. He would be even less himself if he did not insist that a botanist be part of the contingent. No one understood better than he, after all, that plant life was vital to the country's economy and strength. We must know, he said as he waved a hand in the direction of the west, what is growing out there. He turned expectantly toward his friend.

Billy agreed that indeed a botanist should be sent. He could not help thinking then of another day in another spring when His Majesty George III had commissioned his new Royal Botanist to explore and evaluate the little-known Florida territory just acquired from Spain. He asked Jefferson if he had found his man.

His companion appeared not to have heard him. He was describing a proposal he had made to the Philosophical Society some ten years before on the subject of engaging a man competent in horticulture to examine the region contained in ascending the Missouri, crossing the Stony Mountains, and descending the nearest river to the Pacific. M. André Michaux, with his professed interest in the vegetation of the New World, had offered his services.

It was now common knowledge that he had barely reached Kentucky when he was overtaken by an order from the Minister of France, then at Philadelphia, to relinquish the expedition. It was widely suspected that Michaux was engaged in some kind of espionage for his government. In any case, the most recent word of him was that he was lying ill of a fever in the sun-baked desert of Madagascar.

André Michaux had visited the Bartrams on several occasions, the first in the summer of 1786. The French naturalist, then official "Botanist to His Most Christian Majesty" Louis XVI, was preoccupied with establishing a botanical garden near New York, "which, for magnificence &c., will surpass anything of the kind in Am. In it he will introduce many exotics and domestic botanical curiosities." So read a local account of his undertaking. He had dined with George Washington at Mount Vernon and "presented him with some very fine cherry stocks." And he had discovered, in 1788, by a waterfall in a high, rocky glen of the Blue Ridge, a plant lost afterward to history for a hundred years.

In 1789, Billy had accompanied Michaux part of the way on a journey toward the south and had told him where in Florida he might find the aromatic starry yellow anise that he himself had discovered with his father near Lake George in the winter of 1766.

Years later, Michaux's son, François, also a botanist, wrote to Billy that "the marks of friendship that you have invariable bestow on my father and me, will be constantly present to my memory."

Billy's question, about whether a botanist had been found, hung in the spring air along with the fragrance of the fruit trees. Jefferson finally answered it. He had found him, he said, and had come this very afternoon to his home to urge him to accept the offer.

William Bartram sat for a while in silence. One word now, he realized, could alter the course of the rest of his life, as a river is altered when a dam is built or when a storm shifts the sand and silt of its bed. Then, not unexpectedly, he told Tom Jefferson that, alas, he felt himself too old a man.

The President, regarding his friend with some amusement, replied that he had anticipated his answer. He begged for more consideration, declaring that he himself was near Billy's age. Then, in a serious vein, he pointed out that Billy's father had not received his appointment from the King until he was older than the son was now, and he had continued to undertake long and arduous botanical tours well past that time.

Billy tried to protest that his father had been sturdier and heartier, but his companion once again appeared not to be listening. Finally he spoke, in his soft Albemarle accent, of riding the swift rapids of the Missouri, of scaling the passes of the great Stonies, and of gazing at last, like some Balboa, upon an unfamiliar ocean.

Only recently, he went on, had he remarked to his daughter Maria that he sensed in her a willingness to withdraw from society more than was prudent. Might he not say the same of his reluctant friend?

Although once he had believed that one could not find happiness in "the marketplace," he now declared that joy must consist of mixing somewhat with the world. After his wife's death, he had remained closely at home until he finally became sensible of the ill effect this seclusion had had upon his mind. It had led, he felt, to an antisocial and misanthropic state; he would not see this occur in Billy's case. Both had too much to give to the world, and both were still sorely needed.

President Thomas Jefferson paused and gazed with a troubled expression at the spring-flowering borders. There was something else on his mind. Although there was no one in sight, he lowered his voice as he turned again to his friend. Privately, he confided, he had another reason for desiring Billy to make the trip.

It was not generally known, but Captain Lewis had, from early life, suffered from hypochondriac depressions. Jefferson himself had observed these from time to time, and while they were not severe enough to cause real doubt regarding his ability as leader of the expedition, since he was at his best when engaged in physical activity, Tom would nevertheless be glad to have Bartram there to watch over him. The President would be relieved, he added, to offer as counselor for Meriwether a man of Billy's sanguine disposition and faith based on good sense, a man who had not given up morals for mysteries or traded God for Plato.

Then he had leaned forward and placed his hand on Billy's arm. His fine head was bent, but his voice was clear and resonant as he begged his friend to give grave consideration to what had just been asked of him.

When the news of the President's request became known, others were equally eloquent in their persuading. Dr. Benjamin Smith Barton, an old friend from Philadelphia, scientist, professor, and author, wrote to urge Billy: "Come on. You are not too old. You have sufficient youth, health and strength for this journey. You will render great and new services to Natural Science . . . Send your answer by my boy."

"But I have already made my answer," Billy said, looking perplexed.

Ann Bartram was as eager as the rest of the family that her uncle take advantage of the President's offer. "Thy response may have been wrong," she daringly told him. "Thee has been wrong before. Does thee not remember when thee prophesied that Mr. Jefferson would never be famous?"

Billy, who had no recollection of ever having made such a statement, shook his head with increasing bewilderment. To help clear his mind, he took his favorite walk down the path of oak trees that Michaux, whose particular interest this species was, had called "The Dark Walk." One oak among the variety he had named "Bartram's Oak." Here and there between the towering trees, the smaller, graceful Franklinias raised their pale leaves. Billy came at last to the summer-house just beyond the cider mill.

Lichens encroached upon the stones of the press. The flat rock was slippery with moss. Occasional swallows lighted there for a moment, resting between their forays of tilting and swooping down upon the insects that rose from the grasses along the river's edge. Billy never saw those birds without thinking of Linnaeus's theory that the swallows spent the winter underwater.

Peter Kalm, Linnaeus's student and Billy's earliest hero, tended to agree with his master. "It is therefore highly probable, or rather incontestibly true," he wrote, "that Swallows retire in the Northern countries during the winter, into the water, and stay there in a torpid state, till the return of warmth revives them again in the spring."

But when he arrived at "Mr. Bartram's estate," he found that his host "thought that they migrated southward in autumn and returned in spring."

Peter Collinson felt so strongly that his American friend's opinion was the correct one that he brought it to the attention of the Royal Society. If swallows did indeed remain underwater for long periods of time, as Linnaeus argued, then they must possess highly specialized organs to enable them to perform this unusual feat. Where were these organs? He had never heard of them.

He suggested that a logical test of the theory might be the tying of a swallow to a stone, immersing both, and drawing them up after several days. More effective testimony for his migration hypothesis was his statement that two different sea captains of his acquaintance had reported their riggings covered with swallows, as well as other birds, going southward to warmer climes in the fall.

Linnaeus, though, had strong backers in his theory, among them Gilbert White of Selbourne and Dr. Samuel Johnson, and he never retreated from his position. It is reputed, however, that long afterward Dr. Johnson erased the controversial statement from his copy of Linnaeus's *Regnum Animale*.

John Bartram had explained to Collinson his disagreement with the great Linné. Animals, he had always believed, had an instinctive intelligence of their own. He wrote to his friend: "I also am of opinion that the creatures commonly called brutes possess higher qualifications, and more exalted ideas, than our traditional mystery mongers are willing to allow them."

His son Billy inherited his father's conviction and, with his poetic and optimistic outlook, went a step further. In his long observation of animal behavior in the field, a behavior that he believed proceeded from the same causes as man's, he had become convinced of their intuitive knowledge and their ability to communicate this to one another within the species. If they had language, therefore, it was self-evident that they had ideas and understanding. The "Sovereign Creator" had fashioned all animals. Being manifestations of the divine spirit, they must be essentially good.

"Birds are in general social and benevolent creatures," he wrote; "intelligent, ingenious, volatile, active beings; and this order of animal creation consists of various nations, bands, or tribes, as may be observed from their different structure, manner, languages, or voice; each nation, though subdivided into many different tribes, retaining its general form or structure, a similarity of customs, and a sort of dialect or language, particular to that nation or genus from which those tribes seem to have descended or separated." His study of Indians and their ways had certainly influenced his descriptions of bird behavior. In any case, he never lost his belief in the basic dignity of all the inhabitants of God's world.

It has been argued that Billy, besides being poetic and

optimistic, was also romantic and sentimental. He has been called a Romantic Primitive. And his philosophy did, in many ways, reflect the humanitarian and neoclassic spirit of the eighteenth century. But Billy's arguments never failed to be based upon highly accurate and firsthand observations. In this he had, once again, the example of his father to guide him.

John had long been fascinated with the migration of birds, noting when they arrived and departed in his garden, and whether they came singly or in flocks, seemed to follow riverways or mountain ranges, flew high or low, fed on the ground or in flight.

George Edwards, the British ornithologist and friend of Peter Collinson's, in his book *A Natural History of Birds* published in the middle of the eighteenth century, had written: "It would be very proper for all Travellers into foreign Parts, to take notice of what Birds and Beasts they find, and at what Seasons of the Year they find them, and at what Times they disappear, and when they appear again." If he had an opinion on the hibernation of swallows, it was not cited.

Billy believed that the wind was a determining factor in the swallows' migration. He wrote that it was "observable that they always avail themselves of the advantage of high and favorable winds, which likewise do all birds of passage. The pewit, or black cap flycatcher of Catesby [eastern phoebe] is the first bird of passage which appears in the spring in Pennsylvania, which is generally about the first, or middle of March; and then wherever they appear, we may plant peas and beans in the open grounds . . . without fear or danger from frosts."

Less practically and more romantically, he added this: "In the spring of the year the small birds of passage appear very suddenly in Pennsylvania, which is not a little surprising, and no less pleasing: at once the woods, the groves, and meads, are filled with their melody, as if they dropped down from the skies. The reason or probable cause is their setting off with high and fair winds from the southward; for a strong south and southwest wind about the beginning of April never fails bringing millions of these welcome visitors . . ."

There is no doubt that young Billy had studied Mark Catesby's *Natural History of Carolina,* the book that Catesby had sent to John Bartram in exchange for his plant specimens. In his reports to Dr. Fothergill, Billy used Catesby's nomenclature to identify the birds he saw. Like Tom Jefferson, who had used Catesby's notes in his listing of Virginia birds, Billy admired Catesby's art and called his representations "well-figured."

Although Catesby's work was considered the finest natural history of America in its time, actually perhaps the only one, it had its faults. "His drawings are better as to form and attitude, than coloring, which is generally too high," Jefferson told Billy. He suggested to his friend that he publish his own volume of drawings of American birds. "Every page of the *Travels* resounds with their singing," he said.

Billy realized that this would mean the undertaking of another extensive journey into the wilderness. Still, the idea of a book devoted entirely to New World birds did not leave his mind. Because of his list of some two hundred and fifteen avian species, as well as his notes and observations, Billy was generally considered the foremost, if not the sole, productive American ornithologist.

Typically, at the end of his listing, Billy had written: "I am convinced that there are yet several kinds of land birds, and a great number of aquatic fowl that have not come under my particular notice, therefore shall leave them to the investigation of future travelling naturalists of greater ability and industry."

At about the same time that Thomas Jefferson was urging Billy to join his westward expedition, a "travelling naturalist" of a different sort had arrived at Gray's Ferry. He had been hired as a schoolmaster, and he wasted no time in introducing himself to the distinguished Mr. Bartram. To the garden where Presidents and other statesmen and scientists from both continents had conferred, studied, and relaxed, came a little Scotsman named Alexander Wilson, itinerant weaver, sometime poet, and now a teacher in a school on the banks of the Schuylkill.

He had been born in Paisley, not far from the River Clyde, in 1766, the son of a smuggler. As a boy he had herded sheep, but he soon lost his job because he watched birds instead of his flocks. He learned weaving, but, finding that too confining, he became a migrant peddler, selling ribbons and lace, and ballads reminiscent of Robert Burns.

In 1794 he came to America with just the clothes he was wearing and a gun. While walking from Newcastle to Philadelphia, he shot his first New World bird, the redheaded woodpecker, in a woods near the Delaware River. He thought it the most beautiful bird that he had ever seen, and he made a careful drawing of it. This spurred him on to draw the other nameless birds that he saw on his way to the city, and soon he had quite a collection. As he desperately needed work, he obtained, probably somewhat to his surprise, the position of schoolmaster in the little boat-landing community near Kingsessing.

He could not have been there long before he heard of Mr. William Bartram, and he forthwith bundled up his drawings and went to call upon him.

Doubtless, he was amazed at what he found. Billy's room has been compared to a zoo or a Noah's Ark with a colony of resident animals, including the inevitable pet crow that Billy had reared from the nest and whose behavior he was recording. There was also an opossum and a mouse, snakes and frogs and salamanders in cages, birds mounted with their nests and eggs, pinned butterflies and moths, notebooks and illustrations—the whole resembling a young naturalist's dream.

And far from being remote and unapproachable, the great man was enthusiastically engaged in caring for his collection, many of the animals having been brought to him by schoolchildren, and he welcomed the stranger with his customary easy grace and sweet smile.

When he saw Wilson's drawings, his expression deepened; his soft eyes took on a faraway look and his mouth became grave. Here surely was the man to compile the book that Mr. Jefferson had dreamed of: the first American ornithology. Tentatively he suggested it to his guest.

He hardly expected the response to be one of amusement. "But, Mr. Bartram, I cannot even identify these I have drawn. I do not know whether they are sparrow, finch, or thrush. Be pleased to mark the names of each with a pencil."

By the end of that summer, most of it spent in John Bartram's garden, Alexander Wilson had mastered the names and songs of all the native birds. He had counted fifty-one pairs nesting in what he called the "Little Paradise." Totally dependent upon Billy and under his tireless tutelage, he had learned to portray his birds as if drawn from life rather than from mounted figures, to make the little feet appear to be grasping the branch, to show the wings spread in balance, the mouth open to devour the insect, the eye bright and intent. Where Catesby's drawings had a posed, stylistic, museum elegance, Wilson's had the lifelike feeling of having been caught in their natural environment. It was the first time that such an effect had been attempted.

Wilson was well aware of the debt he owed to Billy. His

mentor's opinions and corrections he valued "beyond those of anybody else."

"None," he wrote to him later, "have bestowed such minute observations on the subject as you yourself have done. Indeed they have done little more than copied your nomenclature and observation, and referred to your authority."

Nevertheless, Billy was sufficiently impressed by his pupil's work to write to his friend President Jefferson.

Tom Jefferson had never relinquished his dream of having William Bartram represent him on an expedition into his still largely unknown western acquisition. With no trained naturalist to accompany them, Meriwether Lewis and William Clark had had to do all the collecting and recording of flora and fauna themselves. Although Jefferson had given them detailed instructions, the men lacked either the interest or the time to gather the material Jefferson longed for. Now, in 1806, another expedition was to be launched, to the Arkansas and Red Rivers. Would not Mr. Bartram take into consideration the President's deep disappointment over the lack of biological data previously procured and consent to make this journey?

If Billy had believed himself too old and infirm before, it is not likely that he pondered this decision very long. In February of 1806 he wrote to Jefferson, again declining, but adding: "This very flattering mark of Your Goodness & regard for me, has made a deep empression on my Mind, & will not be effaced, from a Heart most sincerely attached." Then he took the liberty of suggesting Alexander Wilson for the position and told Wilson what he had done.

Imagine the joy and excitement of the little Scotsman upon hearing such news. He had already sent Mr. Jefferson, whom he greatly admired, some of his work and had had a letter in return thanking him for his "elegant drawings."

Now Billy encouraged him to be in touch with the President again and to write that his friend Mr. Bartram, "being near seventy, and the weakness of his eyesight; and apprehensive of his inability to encounter the fatigues and privations un- avoidable in so extensive a tour," he himself would be will- ing to offer his services in his place.

Apparently the letters were never received. In any case, Wilson did not hear from the President and temporarily abandoned his plans for a bird-hunting expedition.

Billy was distressed. He could not help seeing his own boyhood self in this eager, poetic, thwarted young man, confined within the walls of his schoolroom when he longed to be drawing all the birds in America.

The money to finance his trip must somehow be raised. Wilson should prepare a prospectus and folio of his draw- ings and seek subscriptions for a proposed ornithology. One of his first subscribers in that fall of 1807 was Thomas Jefferson.

The next year the first volume of the *American Ornithol- ogy* was published by Samuel Bradford in Philadelphia. With the copy that Wilson gave to William Bartram he had written: "Accept my best wishes for your happiness; wishes as sincere as ever one human being breathed for the happi- ness of another . . . These few specimens . . . may yet tell posterity that I was honored with your friendship, and that to your inspiration they owe their existence."

Billy must have watched his protégé finally leave for his trek into the wilderness with a mixture of gratification, nostalgia, and longing. Most of all, he must have seen himself all over again, freed from captivity, able at last to wander where he would, following every impulse, yet always with a project to pursue and a dream to fulfill.

With him, Wilson took only one comrade, and he was a

strange one. On his shoulder, or wrapped in a handkerchief in his pocket, traveled a little parrot, the Carolina parakeet which he had tamed. Mark Catesby had first described it. The Bartrams had seen hundreds of these jewel-colored birds in the southeast, circling in noisy flocks and hovering over the cypress fruit, their favorite food. "They are easily tamed, when they become docile and familiar," Billy had noted.

The weaver, turned reluctant schoolmaster (he did not whip his pupils sufficiently, their parents protested), enjoyed the fellowship of his small bird. So did the Indians he met on the trails. He wrote of this to William Bartram, adding that to relieve his loneliness he often played Scottish airs on his flute. "Amusement blended with instruction, and a wish to draw the attention of my fellow-citizens, occasionally, from the discordant jarrings of politics to a contemplation of this grandeur, harmony and wonderful variety of Nature exhibited in this beautiful portion of the animal kingdom, have been my principal, and I might say, almost my only motives."

No one understood this better than Billy. And when Wilson returned from a second trip in 1811, Billy invited him to spend the summer with him at Kingsessing. Nancy had been married a few years before to a printer named Robert Carr, and they were helping Billy's younger brother, John, now sixty-eight, with the garden.

Wilson gratefully accepted the invitation. His admiration for William Bartram had never ebbed. As Billy's father had traveled with Billy in spirit, so Billy had traveled with Alexander Wilson. "Few Americans have seen more of their country than I have," he told him, "and none love it more. With the possible exception of one man," he had added, "and he was my constant companion."

To others, he said that because of Bartram "I see new beauties in every bird, plant, or flower I contemplate."

He had many stories to tell, and the Bartrams and Carrs listened enthralled. None was more interesting to Billy than that of a chance encounter in a frontier store in Louisville. Wilson had gone there in search of a possible subscriber. To the handsome young man behind the counter, with its fowling pieces, powder horns, and axes, he displayed his portfolio of drawings. The clerk, after studying them intently, produced a folder of his own bird paintings.

"They were," Wilson told Billy, "more numerous and lively in execution than mine."

The young man, like so many other naturalists, was happy to lock the door of his shop, pick up his fiddle, and lead the itinerant artist with the parakeet on his shoulder to "ransack" the woods and hunt and obtain birds he had never seen before.

"He did not subscribe to my *Ornithology*," Wilson acknowledged, "and I was not surprised. I saw at once that his own drawings were superior."

Bartram inquired the name and education of this artist. "I doubt you'll hear of him," Wilson said a little testily. "He has a wife and a partner and must work in the shop for their support. Science or literature has not one friend in that place. His name was French, I would venture; Audubon, or something of the sort. I have it writ somewhere."

Later that year, when Audubon returned Wilson's call, the dour Scot, as he was sometimes nicknamed, hurried him off at once to Peale's Museum, where one of Willson Peale's sons, Rembrandt, was working in an exhibition room. According to Audubon, Alexander "spoke not of birds or drawings." Even worse, he stolidly refused to introduce the young artist to William Bartram, using as an excuse that his benefactor was not strong enough to receive strangers. When

Billy reprimanded him for this, Wilson repeated: "He did not subscribe to my *Ornithology*."

Others did, though; five hundred sets were sold at $120 each. Besides Jefferson, most of his cabinet bought them; so did De Witt Clinton, Robert Fulton, Benjamin West, Rufus King, and many colleges, libraries, and plantations. Wilson's *American Ornithology*, the first work of its kind ever to be published, had reached nine volumes, and the tenth was in progress, when its author died suddenly at the age of forty-seven. A cold, suffered while in a weakened condition from strain and overwork, was reported as the cause of death.

Billy had another theory. "While men do not die of disappointment alone," he told his niece, "it contributes to the giving up of the ghost. Thee sees, Mr. Wilson desired to be better than he was, and he could not be."

Although on approaching seventy Billy thought of himself as elderly, his interests were those of a younger man. An elected member of the American Philosophical Society, he maintained valuable friendships through correspondence and visitors to the garden, in which he still worked almost daily. Such guests as Alexander Hamilton and James Madison were never surprised to find him hoeing and weeding. Often his pet crow, "a bird of a happy temperament," sat on a nearby branch or flew to his head or shoulder. Billy had written in his *Anecdotes of an American Crow* that the bird had an innate and incontestable intelligence beyond his training to respond to commands.

Tom Jefferson, now completing his second term as President, never lost his love for Wilson's "Little Paradise" and came to the garden whenever he could. In the fall of 1809 he sent word to Billy of the death, "under symptoms of derangement," of Meriwether Lewis. "About three o'clock in the night he did the deed which plunged his friends into affliction, and deprived his country of one of her most valued citizens," he wrote with deep sadness.

There was no doubt that Jefferson was longing to retire to his hilltop farm. He never failed to mention it to Bartram. "No occupation is so delightful to me as the culture of the earth," he wrote. "Though an old man, I am but a young gardener."

Other visitors, not so well known, also arrived at the garden. In 1801, a young Yorkshireman from West Riding sailed to Philadelphia. A printer by trade, he found far more delight in birds and plants. It was natural that he be drawn to the Academy of Sciences. There Dr. Benjamin Smith Barton took an immediate interest in him and hastened to introduce him to William Bartram. Thus it was that Thomas Nuttall came for the first time to Kingsessing.

There it is quite likely that he met another Thomas, young Tom Say of Gray's Ferry, Billy's grandnephew. It was for Tom's grandfather that the eastern phoebe, *Sayornis phoebe,* had been named by John Latham, a British ornithologist who, in his systematic handbook, *A General Synopsis of Birds,* had described for the first time two dozen American birds.

Years later, in the first volume of his definitive work, *A Manual of the Ornithology of the United States and Canada,* Nuttall was to write of the phoebe: "According to the touching relation of Wilson, this humble and inoffensive bird forms conjugal attachments which probably continue through life; for, like the faithful Bluebirds, a pair continued for several years to frequent and build in a romantic cave in the forest which made part of the estate of the venerable naturalist, William Bartram." Thus, in a way, four pioneers of American ornithology were joined by a single sentence.

Tom Say, whose family was held in high esteem by Jefferson for its character "as well as a respect for Mr. Bartram's friendships," picked up shells and collected insects along the banks of Schuylkill, where he lived. These specimens he took to show to his great-uncle who praised them and encouraged him to collect more. Later, Tom Say was to become known as the Father of American Conchology and Entomology.

As for Thomas Nuttall, he never tired of listening to Billy's accounts of his travels in the Carolinas and Georgia, and, urged on by his "venerable" friend, he undertook, in the late summer of 1815, a trip that followed many of the Bartram trails.

The Great Smokies fascinated him. The same mists rising from the coves and trailing across the mountains that had enchanted Billy enchanted him too. The same bright water-falls and dark pools beguiled him, and the wild flowers cap-tured his imagination as much as did the birds. Always in his mind were those in whose footsteps he followed: William Bartram and the two Michaux.

On his protégé's return, Billy listened to every word, re-living his own travels. He felt old and frail now, although he worked every day in his father's garden, wearing, a visitor reported, "an old hat which flapped over his face; a coarse shirt . . . his waistcoat and breeches were both of leather, and his shoes were tied with leather string." His younger brother John had died in 1812. Ann, or Nancy as he still called her, and her husband, Colonel Carr, a hero of the recent war with Britain, whose military commission Billy had endorsed, had undertaken the management of the gar-den. Carr, with his brother, had printed a sixty-three-page *Catalogue* of the plants. And Ann herself was an experienced botanist and artist, having been taught by Alexander Wilson as well as by her uncle. "May the venerable groves and splendid and curious trees of this patriarchal residence long survive the waning existence of its present proprietors!" Nuttall wrote.

Nuttall was to travel farther than the Bartrams, as far as

the distant Pacific, and become the first naturalist to see the high mountain meadows of the west, carpeted with blooms, and to give these plants their scientific names. On his return from one of his excursions he hastened to Kingsessing to report to his beloved friend and to work again in the study where he had spent so much time writing that it was now called "Nuttall's room." Ann Bartram Carr met him on the porch, whose stones her grandfather had carved. "Your room awaits you, Mr. Nuttall," she said. "But Uncle Billy is no longer here."

It had been a warm morning in that July of 1823. William Bartram sat at his desk writing a description of a plant. Through the open window he could hear his favorite brown thrasher calling to him from its perch in the great cypress tree his father had planted. "A highly intelligent bird," Billy remarked to his nephew-in-law, Robert Carr, who had come in and was listening too. "I have good reason to believe that it is the same one which returns each summer."

"There is a man here in this state at Mill Grove," Colonel Carr told him, "who has actually proved for the first time that birds do seek out their old nesting places. He captured a pair of phoebes nesting beneath a bridge and attached tiny metal rings to their legs. This spring, when the birds arrived, they were wearing his bands. The man's name is Audubon. He's a bird artist and was an acquaintance of Mr. Wilson's, I believe."

When Carr had left, Billy sat contemplating what he had said. Like rivers, phoebes also seemed to have played a part in his life. He was not at all surprised to hear they returned to their homes.

He thought of the tanager in the tulip tree and of the boy who had believed even then that the same birds came back. He peered from the window to see where his thrasher sang.

A pale haze of heat hung over the river, softening its glare and gilding the distant meadows, shutting out the houses that had sprung up on the farther bank. It restored to the scene its earlier look; it appeared much as it had when his father worked in his garden and Mr. Franklin would arrive unannounced on the path. And there was his father now, hoeing his flower bed in the hot sun.

'But it's too warm for him to be working,' Billy worried. 'I must go and tell him so.' He rose from his desk, and it seemed that all the birds were singing. "I must go," he said.

"But he has not gone," Thomas Jefferson, in his eighties now, wrote to comfort Nancy. "Though his spirit with its kindred, the just, the good, the beloved of men, is in the bosom of his God, he remains everywhere around you. When you wish to find him, you have only to look in his garden, and in his work, and in his green world. Like myself, he had ever dreaded a doting old age. If it is permitted to the dead to watch over the things of this world, you may be certain that he will watch over you."

And he might then have added what was said of himself, four years later, in a eulogy before the American Philosophical Society: "The grief that such a man is dead, may well be assuaged by the proud consolation that such a man has lived."

CHAPTER 8

THE GARDEN GROWS

"Hills peep o'er hills, and Alps on Alps arise!"

Alexander Pope

The knocking persisted until it was no longer possible to ignore it. In a sort of trance, the young poet laid down his pen, turned over his page as was his custom when interrupted, and opened the door. A wafting of fresh air from the sea flowed past him into his study. He pressed his hand to his forehead. He had not been feeling well of late, and the night before, he had slept badly, with strange, drug-induced dreams.

But the cool air revived him. He took a clear look at his visitor, who, he was perplexed to see, was a total stranger to him.

"Mr. Coleridge, I come from Porlock on urgent business."

Samuel Taylor Coleridge stared at the bill in the stranger's hand with a kind of wild-eyed despair. Was it possible that for this he had been disturbed at his morning's work?

"It is long overdue," the stranger said, as if in reply.

The bill was discussed at some length and finally paid. The intruder continued on his way; the poet returned to his table. He picked up his half-blank page to read:

For he on honey-dew hath fed,
And drunk the milk of Paradise.

The lines filled him with bewilderment. They might as well have been written by someone else, for what did they mean? Who had fed on honey-dew and drunk the milk of Paradise? He had fragmentary recollections of a vision; what had it been?

It was as though somebody, perhaps that wretched fellow from Porlock, had cast a stone onto the surface of his mind's stream and scattered all the images mirrored there. Only in this case, with the calming of the waters, no unruffled reflection reappeared.

The bell in the steeple of Culbone Church sounded twelve times. The morning was gone. Coleridge looked from his window to the northwest, where, beyond the empty reaches of Exmoor, the Bristol Channel shone mildly in the summer sun. There was no one in sight. A few sheep grazed; a pair of lapwings circled and lighted in the furze—that was all. He had expected when he chose this lonely Brimstone farmhouse in Somerset that he would have few if any interruptions.

The year was 1797. Coleridge had been in poor health and, consequently, poor spirits for several years. While in school he had contracted rheumatic fever, and recently he had been troubled with insomnia and toothache. Unexplained pains came and went in various parts of his body. The previous night, or perhaps early in the morning—he was not certain exactly when because he had been absorbed in a book he was reading—he had taken an anodyne prescribed by his physician and had fallen asleep in his chair, "a sleep of the external senses" he called it.

Later he wrote to his brother: "Laudanum gave me repose, not sleep; but you, I believe, know how divine that repose is, what a spot of enchantment, a green spot of fountain and flowers and trees in the very heart of a waste of sands." The images have a familiar sound.

He turned to his table where two volumes lay. One was entitled *Purchas's Pilgrimage*. It described, Coleridge remembered then, the ordering by the Khan Kubla of a palace to be built in a vast, stately garden.

The other book was the work of an American named Bartram, the second edition of his *Travels*, published a few years before in London. To the young poet, restless and unhappy at home, it had opened up a new world. He had even dreamed of sailing to the Schuylkill to write there among the "insense-bearing" trees and the "sunny spots of greenery" that his mind, with true poetic license, transplanted from Florida to Pennsylvania.

Coleridge had already transformed Bartram's "wondrous" spangled bream and other "most beautiful" fish into the water snakes which "moved in tracks of shining white" and flashed "golden fire" near the becalmed ship of the Ancient Mariner.

The owls and doves and snakes of "Christabel" came from the pages of the *Travels*. The hawk, wreathed round by the whip snake, which Billy observed on his journey from Spalding's Lower Store to Talahasochte, Coleridge used symbolically in three different poems. His notebooks were crowded with Bartram's plants and animals, his sunlight and moonlight and storms, and particularly his beloved springs and fountains. Page after page was copied directly from Bartram.

"Tamaha's stream" in "Lewti" must surely be the Altamaha River. "Lewti" itself, with its cliffs and clouds, was originally called "The Wild Indian's Love-Chaunt."

In his preface to "Christabel," Coleridge attacked critics "who seem to hold that every possible thought and image is traditional; who have no notion that there are such things as fountains in the world."

And as Billy and his father had been fascinated by the "inchanting and amazing crystal fountain, which incessantly threw up, from the dark rocky caverns below, tons of water every minute, forming . . . a creek . . . which meanders six miles through green meadows," so the author of "Kubla Khan" wrote of "a mighty fountain" which "flung up momently the sacred river. Five miles meandering" until it reached "the caverns measureless to man." Schoolboys who have never heard of either of the Bartrams memorize the familiar lines.

Two years before his writing of the never-completed "Kubla Khan," or, as he called it, "A Vision in a Dream: A Fragment," Coleridge had met a fellow poet, William Wordsworth. To him Coleridge introduced Bartram's work as "not a Book of Travels properly speaking, but a series of poems, chiefly descriptive, occasioned by the objects which the Traveller observed."

One does not have to read far into Wordsworth to realize that he too fell rapidly under the spell of Billy Bartram. His famous daffodils sound very like Bartram's "vegetable beauties" which "by the mountain breezes are tossed about." The long poem "Ruth," written while in Germany with Coleridge, tells of a "Youth from Georgia's shore—

> *A military casque he wore*
> *With splendid feathers drest;*
> *He brought them from the Cherokees;*
> *The feathers nodded in the breeze,*
> *And made a gallant crest.*

Can there be any doubt that Wordsworth had seen Billy's drawing of Mico Chlucco, chief of the Seminoles, the frontispiece of the *Travels?*

He told of girls—a happy rout!
Who quit their fold with dance and shout,
Their pleasant Indian town,
To gather strawberries all day long;

He told of the magnolia spread
High as a cloud, high overhead!
The cypress and her spire;
—Of flowers that with one scarlet gleam
Cover a hundred leagues, and seem
To set the hills on fire.

It is certainly Bartram all over again, as are these lines from *The Prelude* describing

a haunt
In which the heron should delight to feed
By the shy rivers, and the pelican
Upon the cypress spire in lonely thought
Might sit and sun himself.

Compare this with Billy's early trip on the Altamaha, resounding with the call of the heron, and the sighting "on yon decayed, defoliated Cypress tree, the solitary wood-pelican, dejectedly perched upon its utmost elevated spire . . ."

Birds and plants that the poet had never seen he glimpsed through Billy's eyes. His descriptions of birds already known to him were enhanced by the *Travels*. As did Coleridge, so Wordsworth drew upon Bartram's owls. In *The Prelude* the boy of Winander

Blew mimic hootings to the silent owls,
That they might answer him; and they would shout
Across the watery vale, and shout again,
Responsive to his call, with quivering peals,
And long halloos and screams, and echoes loud . . .

This cannot help recalling Billy's description: "I was awakened and greatly surprised by the terrifying screams of Owls . . . screaming and shouting, which increased and spread every way for miles around, in dreadful peals vibrating through the dark extensive forests, meadows and lakes."

But beyond the poetic images, Wordsworth caught Billy's philosophy, "voyaging through strange seas of thought alone," with "meditation slipping in between the beauty coming and the beauty gone."

> *His daily teachers had been woods and rills,*
> *The silence that is in the starry sky,*
> *The sleep that is among the lonely hills.*

And as we read still further, can we not picture the young Billy gazing with longing through the windows of Mr. Thomson's schoolroom?

> *One impulse from the vernal wood*
> *May teach you more of man,*
> *Of moral evil and of good,*
> *Than all the sages can.*

Like Bartram, Wordsworth was a true product of the eighteenth century and of his own particular environment.

Robert Southey, the Poet Laureate of England and friend of Wordsworth and Coleridge, read the *Travels* and borrowed from its subtropical birds and plants. His epic poem *Madoc*, published in 1805, portrays a wild turkey in a magnolia tree in Florida.

The Vicomte de Chateaubriand came from France to Philadelphia in 1791 to see the New World and eventually to write an epic on the American Indian. He traveled for a while in the wildernesses of Pennsylvania and New York, often in the company of Cayugas and Onandagas, but he never saw the southern companions of Billy Bartram. Just the same, he called his prose poem *Atala*, a name reminiscent of Billy's "Alatamaha," and he depicted wild strawberries, magnolias, live oaks, and southeastern plants and animals he could have seen nowhere but in the pages of the *Travels*. In fact, he once admitted that he had so mixed up his own notes with notations from the *Travels* that he could hardly remember which was which.

Britain and the Continent, in the surge of a Romantic revolution and already inspired by the concept of the noble savage and the unexplored landscape across the seas, read and wrote all that they could, gleaning freely from Bartram. Thus, as once John's seeds had crossed the ocean and influenced a generation of gardeners, so half a century later did his son's words traverse the same ocean to excite readers and writers alike.

And at home, where the famous garden continued to grow, tended now and added to extensively by Nancy and her husband, Colonel Robert Carr, what was the influence there? Visitors continued to come to see the plantings. Colonel Carr classified the nursery and sent specimens abroad. "From this nursery," reported the Pennsylvania Horticultural Society in 1850, "many thousands of plants and seeds are exported every season to Europe and South America."

To Caesar A. Rodney, American Minister of the Argentines, Robert Carr wrote from Bartram's Botanic Garden: "I have taken the liberty to forward to you by the brig Clio, a small collection of seeds of North American trees, shrubs & herbaceous plants, hoping they may be acceptable to yourself or some of your botanical friends at Buenos Ayres . . . in return for which I would be happy to receive a few of the seeds of any South American plants . . . I am particularly anxious to obtain seeds or plants of the 'Paraguay tea'."

How reminiscent this is of the correspondence, a century earlier, between John Bartram and Peter Collinson.

Nancy Bartram Carr, whom Thomas Nuttall called "a considerable botanist," and her husband, a printer, published a catalogue of their garden. As early as 1807 Billy and his younger brother John had compiled "A Catalog of Trees, Shrubs and Herbaceous Plants Indigenous to the United States of America, cultivated and Disposed of by John Bartram and Son at their Botanical Garden at Kingsessing, near Philadelphia. To Which is Added a Catalog of Foreign Plants Collected from Various Parts of the Globe."

From the grapes that were his speciality, it was reported that Colonel Carr made "very good wine." In 1763, returning from the south, John Bartram had written to his friend Jared Eliot in Connecticut: "In my journey from Carolina & since, I have thought much of ye cultivation of our native grape . . . if we could raise a sufficient quantity of vines, either by layers, cuttings, or grafting of ye best sorts." Now his granddaughter and her husband were grafting and pruning some of the same ancient vines, gnarled and thick and so strong that they seemed to uphold the very arbor they twined around.

But by 1891, with the Carrs gone, the garden had grown to weeds and tall grass and scattered branches. To save it, the city of Philadelphia bought the land for a park.

Two years later, Bartram descendants formed the John Bartram Association, dedicated to restoring the garden and to repairing and maintaining the house, barns, and tool sheds. The property was opened to the public, and new members outside the family were admitted to the association.

Other nearby places were restored: Stenton, the home of James Logan; the Marshallton estate of Humphrey Marshall, Bartram cousin, botanic gardener, and author of *Arbustrum Americanum*; Joshua and Samuel Pierce's plantation, now Longwood Gardens; and Minshall and Jacob Paynter's house and garden, the present Tyler Arboretum.

The John Bartram Association became a member of the National Trust for the Preservation of Historic Houses and later affiliated with the Garden Club Federation of Pennsylvania. In 1931 a bicentennial celebration was held to commemorate the founding of the garden. But by this time Philadelphia was no longer the botanical center of the New World.

That honor passed to New York with Dr. John Torrey, who, as a small boy, collected plants for a horticulturist in his father's debtors' prison. Later Torrey became Professor of Chemistry and Botany at the New York College of Physicians and Surgeons. With Asa Gray he wrote the *Flora of North America*. When Gray, author of the definitive *Elements of Botany*, moved to Harvard, greater Boston was considered the horticultural center of the United States.

Besides his garden, Billy left to science, and particularly to ornithology, the first comprehensive list of native birds recorded by an American. "Being willing to contribute my mite towards illustrating the subject of the peregrination of the tribes of birds of N. America," he wrote modestly, "I shall subjoin a nomenclature of the birds of passage, agreeable to my observation, when on my travels from New-England to New-Orleans, on the Missiippi, and point of Florida." The birds numbered 215 species. And they were listed according to whether they were year-round residents of either Pennsylvania or the southeast or whether they "peregrinated" in between.

Actually, it was the peregrinations that had concerned Billy far more than the mere listing. From the first day when as a young boy he had wondered about the tanager in the tulip tree, until as an old man he recorded the comings and goings of catbirds in his garden, the mysteries of migration engrossed him as they engross ornithologists young and old today.

In 1875, Elliott Coues told the Academy of Natural Sciences in Philadelphia: "If Wilson was the father of American ornithology, as he has been styled, Bartram, back to whom the pedigree of many names is traceable, was certainly the grandfather of that vigorous offspring." And later he added that he considered the *Travels* the starting point of a distinctively American school of ornithology.

Philadelphia-born Witmer Stone, who, until his death in 1939, spent fifty years with the Academy and has been referred to by Roger Tory Peterson as "one of the great field ornithologists of his time," called Billy's list "a landmark in the progress of American ornithology . . . and the first ornithological contribution, worthy of the name, written by a native American."

Dr. Stone went on to comment upon William Bartram's assistance to others, observing that "most generously and cheerfully did he share his store with those who came to him."

A more recent ornithologist, Dr. H. C. Oberholser, said of Billy: "He did for the birds of the United States what all the naturalists of Europe in a century had not done for theirs."

In *Birds and Men*, Robert H. Welker wrote that "William Bartram, unsystematic though he was in many ways, recognized the principle of interrelationship and evolution among birds, noting that various bird 'tribes' have certain characteristics in common because they have 'descended or separated' from a parent stock."

Dr. Francis Harper, editor of the Naturalist's Edition of the *Travels,* told the Philosophical Society that William Bartram "has left an indelible and altogether priceless record of American natural history in the Eighteenth Century." As recently as 1970 a writer in the *Auk,* official publication of the American Ornithologists' Union, stated: "There is little need to elaborate on the importance of William Bartram in the growth of natural history studies in America."

As John Bartram had had a genus of moss named for him, so his son William was immortalized in taxonomy by his pupil, the itinerant Scottish weaver Alexander Wilson, who designated a shore bird of the fields and meadows "Bartram's Tattler."

The scientific name of the bird is *Bartramia longicauda.* "I have honored it with the name of my very worthy friend, near whose botanic gardens, on the banks of the river Schuylkill, I first found it," Wilson wrote. The bird was once also called "Bartram's Sandpiper," but today we know it as the upland plover, a long-legged, long-necked frequenter of high, cultivated pastures, with a ringing, whistling note and a habit of perching on fence posts.

Once it was relatively common, and every country boy knew its call. But in open locations it was an easy target for hunters, and civilization encroached upon its breeding grounds. In the first quarter of this century Edward Howe Forbush wrote: "Our children's children may never see an Upland Plover in the sky or hear its rich notes on the summer air . . . That long-drawn, rolling, mellow whistle as the bird mounts high in the air has the sad quality of the November wind."

So Billy himself might have described its "seraphic music in the ethereal skies."

Thomas Carlyle wrote to Ralph Waldo Emerson: "Do you know Bartram's *Travels?* Treats of Florida chiefly, has a wonderful kind of floundering eloquence in it; and has grown immeasurably old."

Written by that admittedly strange combination of artist, Quaker, and pantheist, influenced alike by Pope and the Bible, the *Travels* was produced in a style that was strictly Billy's own. As few other similar works, it reflected his character and personality almost completely.

While some critics opposed the "somewhat too luxuriant and poetical language" and Thoreau deplored its "exoticism," many agreed that the vivacious and effortless lyric quality of the prose, the sensitivity and awe, the new innocence and joy, and particularly the aesthetic fervor of the writer more than atoned for any quaint or stilted diction, or artificial devices of style. "William Bartram," wrote the Coleridge scholar John Livingston Lowes, "exemplified that rarest of combinations: the mind of a scientist with the soul of a poet."

Audubon, who had not been allowed to meet him, read him with a "thrill of delight."

Compared with today's tendency toward a distilled scientific effect in writing, Billy Bartram emerges as what he also was, a romantic, concerned with the remote as well as the immediate, the storm as much as the calm, the unknown along with the known.

Aldous Huxley has said: "The proper study of mankind is Man, and next to Man, mankind's properist study is Nature, that Nature of which he is an emergent part and with which . . . he must learn to live in harmony." That Billy lived in harmony not only with nature but also with his fellows and himself is evident on nearly every page he wrote.

Sometimes the accuracy of his descriptions was ques-

tioned. In 1793 a reviewer in London objected to the use of
the term "crocodile" for "alligator, as he indiscriminately
terms that horrid animal." But in a footnote Billy had already explained why he had done that, "alligator being the
country name."

Others criticized Billy's inclusion of "tygers" in the southeast. Yet in another footnote he had made it plain: "This
creature is called, in Pennsylvania and the northern States,
Panther; but in Carolina and the southern States, is called
Tyger."

His "painted vulture" also aroused ornithological doubts.
"For years scientists discounted William Bartram's description of what must have been the king vulture in Florida,"
wrote Helen Gere Cruickshank, who painstakingly and intel-
ligently followed the Bartram trail. "Knowing how quickly a
species can disappear from an area, few now doubt that king
vultures were observed by Bartram."

Dr. Francis Harper also testifies to the "soundness and
accuracy of his [Bartram's] observations on plants, animals,
and Indians. There can be no question," he asserts, "of his
fundamental integrity as a naturalist."

'Tis God alone, Almighty Lord,
The Holy One by me Ador'd.

Since 1770 Billy had seen these words carved by his father
and set above the window. And he had heard John Bartram
say: "Vast are the bodies which roll in the immense expanse;
orbs beyond orbs without number, suns beyond suns, systems beyond systems. How can we look at these without
amazement, or contemplate the Divine Majesty that rules
them without the most humble adoration?"

"He seems to have been designed for the study and contemplation of Nature," Billy once said about his father. Like

the father, the son was comparably designed. They seem to resemble two trees, an oak and a willow, growing side by side in the garden.

Do the trees still cast their shadows? In 1931, at the bicentennial celebration of the founding of the garden, Professor Rodney True said of John: "He did two things that made his name known, even to our present day; he added greatly to mankind's store of knowledge and . . . he planted a garden."

In that garden the Franklinia still flourishes. Not found in the wild for over a century and a half, it borders the path where Benjamin Franklin walked to find John hoeing his flower bed while Billy, a truant from haying, hid and sketched. "It is so hardy," wrote William Bartram of the tree his father had described, "as to stand in an open exposed situation in the Garden in Pennsylvania without suffering the least injury from our most severe frosts, when very few Plants from that country will do in our Green houses."

And, typically, as he offered his specimens and drawings to the British Museum, where they remain to this day, he asked for "no other gratuity than the bare mention of my being the discoverer." But "with a perfect sense of gratitude," he added, "I with pleasure acknowledge that the Noble Fothergill liberally supported me whilst in his employ with ample pecuniary assistance."

On August 23, 1969, across the continent in Seattle, an American postage stamp commemorating the meeting of the Eleventh International Botanical Congress was issued. It portrayed the *Franklinia alatamaha,* representing the southeast. Since the tree no longer grows where it was found, this must be construed as a tribute to the man for whom it was named. Who can deny that it is at the same time a tribute to the two men who stood in the light of a fall afternoon by the

edge of a strange river and found a plant theretofore unknown to science?

Not one of the trees growing in the garden today is believed to have been planted by John Bartram. The cypress
which he brought from the land of the Delawares as a
switch in his boot, and which by 1895 had expanded to nine
feet in diameter, is no longer there and has been replaced by
a smaller cypress. Lady Petre's pear tree put out no new
leaves after 1931.

But the garden is still green. Birds still sing in the tall
trees. The "Hidden River" still flows past the old rock trough
and cider-mill stone. On the riverbank there are factories
now; their whistles mingle with the calling of the birds.
Buildings have sprung up along the shore, and it is difficult
to make out the distant Delaware. A city park borders one
side of the garden. Boys of twelve or fourteen, resembling
the young Billy, with long hair and shirts open at the neck,
slip through the hedge to look around.

In 1731, the year of the founding of the garden, John
wrote to Reverend Eliot: "I have split rocks seventeen feet
long and built four houses of hewn stone split out of the rock
with my own hands." The buildings are there today. The
John Bartram Association, which maintains them, receives
visitors who come from around the world to see the house
and garden on the Schuylkill.

Emily Read Cheston, writing eloquently of the father,
said that the "simple, wholesome, powerful personality of
John Bartram still pervades the Garden in which he pursued
his labor of love more than two centuries ago."

Of his son, it is hardly too much to say that his "restless
spirit of curiosity" pervades not only the garden but also all
those "natural secrets, arts, and sciences" of his father's
philosophy. Through them, Billy Bartram has shared for all
time the wonders of his green world.

Chronology

❧

1739   William Bartram is born on April 20 to John Bartram and Ann Mendenhall Bartram in Kingsessing, Pennsylvania.

1740   Tom Robeson is born in North Carolina.

1742   Lord Petre, John Bartram's first patron, dies of smallpox in England at the age of twenty-nine.

1743   Thomas Jefferson is born in Virginia.
Colonel William Bartram, Billy's uncle, buys the plantation, Ashwood, on the Cape Fear River in North Carolina.

1744   Benjamin Franklin forms the American Philosophical Society, with John Bartram as charter member.

1749   Peter Kalm comes to John Bartram's garden.

1753   Billy Bartram travels with his father to visit Cadwallader Colden in New York.

1755   Billy travels with his father to Connecticut to visit the Reverend Jared Eliot.

1757   Billy goes for the first time to Ashwood.

1760   George III becomes King of England at the age of twenty-two.

1761   Billy returns to Ashwood to go into business in North Carolina.

1763   England acquires the territory of Florida from Spain.
Mary Bartram marries Tom Robeson.

1765   John Bartram is appointed Royal Botanist to King George.
John and Billy Bartram discover the Franklinia in Georgia.

1766 Alexander Wilson is born in Scotland.

1768 Peter Collinson dies in England.

1770 Colonel William Bartram dies in North Carolina.

1771 Billy's cousin, Dr. William Bartram, dies in North Carolina in a yellow-fever epidemic.

1772 Billy's aunt, Elizabeth Bartram, dies in North Carolina.

1773 Under the patronage of Dr. John Fothergill of London, Billy begins his exploration of the southeast.

1775 The American Revolution begins with the Battles of Lexington and Concord.
Billy reaches the Mississippi River.

1776 The Revolution begins in the south with the Battle of Moore's Creek Bridge.
Thomas Jefferson drafts and signs the Declaration of Independence.
Billy visits his cousin Mary for the last time.

1777 Billy arrives home in Kingsessing in January.
John Bartram dies in September at the age of seventy-eight.

1779 Billy's cousin, Sarah Bartram Brown, dies in North Carolina.

1780 Dr. John Fothergill dies in England at sixty-eight.

1781 Tom Robeson leads the Whigs to victory at the "Tory Hole" in the Battle of Elizabethtown.

1782 For reasons of poor health, Billy is forced to decline an offer from the University of the State of Pennsylvania to be Professor of Botany.

1784 Ann Mendenhall Bartram, Billy's mother, dies at eighty-seven.

1785 Colonel Thomas Robeson, Jr., dies in North Carolina at forty-five.
John James Audubon is born in Santo Domingo.
Humphrey Marshall, cousin of John Bartram, publishes *Arbustrum Americanum,* containing the first description of the *Franklinia alatamaha.*

1786 Thomas Nuttall is born in England.
Billy is elected to membership in the American Philosophical Society.

1787 Robeson County, named for Tom, is founded in North Carolina.

1789 George Washington becomes the first President of the United States.

1790 Benjamin Franklin dies at eighty-four.

1791 The *Travels* are published in Philadelphia.
Dr. Alexander Garden dies at sixty-two.

1792   The *Travels* are published in London.
        Henry Laurens dies in South Carolina.
1793   Thomas Jefferson takes a house in the country near Kingsessing
        for the summer.
1794   A second edition of the *Travels* is published in London.
        Peter Robeson, Tom's brother, dies.
1795   Michael Collinson dies at sixty-five.
1797   Samuel Taylor Coleridge writes "Kubla Khan."
1799   Mary Bartram Robeson Morehead dies in North Carolina.
        George Washington dies at Mount Vernon.
1801   Thomas Jefferson becomes President.
        Thomas Nuttall arrives in Philadelphia and meets Billy.
1802   Alexander Wilson comes to Bartram's garden.
1804   The Lewis and Clark expedition sets out on the "Missourie"
        for the Far West.
1807   Billy and his brother John publish a catalogue of their garden.
1808   Charles Willson Peale paints Billy's portrait.
        Volume I of Alexander Wilson's *Ornithology* is published in
        Philadelphia.
1809   Billy's niece, Ann (Nancy) Bartram, marries Robert Carr.
        Meriwether Lewis dies at thirty-five on the Natchez Trace.
1810   Wilson meets Audubon in Kentucky.
        Billy's great-nephew, Tom Say, comes to the garden.
1812   John Bartram, Jr., dies at sixty-nine.
1813   Alexander Wilson dies in Philadelphia at forty-seven.
1814   General Thomas Brown, husband of Billy's cousin Sarah, dies
        in North Carolina.
1823   William Bartram dies at Kingsessing on July 22 at the age of
        eighty-four.

Bibliography

≫≪

Of all the material which I read in connection with this work, I found the following to be of particular interest and value.

THE BARTRAMS

Cheston, Emily Read, *John Bartram*. Philadelphia: The John Bartram Association, 1938.

Cruickshank, Helen G., *John & William Bartram's America*. New York: The Devin-Adair Company, 1957.

Darlington, William, *Memorials of John Bartram and Humphrey Marshall*. Philadelphia: Lindsay & Blakiston, 1849.

Earnest, Ernest, *John and William Bartram*. Philadelphia: University of Pennsylvania Press, 1940.

Ewan, Joseph, *William Bartram: Botanical and Zoological Drawings, 1756–1788*. Philadelphia: American Philosophical Society, 1968.

Fagin, N. Bryllion, *William Bartram: Interpreter of the American Landscape*. Baltimore: Johns Hopkins University Press, 1933.

Harper, Francis, *The Travels of William Bartram*, Naturalist's Edition. New Haven: Yale University Press, 1958.

Herbst, Josephine, *New Green World*. New York: Hastings House, 1954.

OTHER NATURALISTS OF THE TIME

Audubon, Maria R., *Audubon and His Journals*. New York: Dover Publications, 1960.

Beebe, William, *The Book of Naturalists*. New York: Alfred A. Knopf, 1945.

Benson, Adolph D., *Peter Kalm's Travels in North America*. New York: Dover Publications, 1966.

Brett-James, Norman G., *The Life of Peter Collinson*. London: Dunstan & Company.

Edwards, George W., "Peter Collinson," *Journal of the Royal Horticultural Society*. London, August 1968.

Frick, G. F. and Stearns, R. P., *Mark Catesby: The Colonial Audubon*. Urbana: University of Illinois Press, 1961.

Graustein, Jeanette E., *Thomas Nuttall, Naturalist*. Cambridge: Harvard University Press, 1967.

Harshberger, John W., *The Botanists of Philadelphia*. Philadelphia, 1899.

Peattie, Donald Culross, *Green Laurels*. New York: Garden City Publishing Company, 1938.

Welker, Robert H., *Birds and Men*. Cambridge: Harvard University Press, 1955.

BENJAMIN FRANKLIN

Franklin, Benjamin, *Autobiography and Other Writings*. Boston: Houghton Mifflin Company, 1958.

Franklin, Benjamin, *Poor Richard's Almanacks*. New York: The Heritage Press, 1964.

Gray, Austin K., *Benjamin Franklin's Library*. New York: The Macmillan Company, 1936.

Labaree, L. W. and Bell, W. J., Jr., *Mr. Franklin*. New Haven: Yale University Press, 1956.

Van Doren, Carl, *Benjamin Franklin*. New York: Viking Press, 1938.

THOMAS JEFFERSON

Boorstin, Daniel J., *The Lost World of Thomas Jefferson*. New York: Henry Holt & Company, 1948.

Padover, Saul K., *Jefferson*. New York: The New American Library, 1952.
———, *A Jefferson Profile*. New York: The John Day Company, 1956.
———, *The Writings of Thomas Jefferson*. New York: The Heritage Press, 1967.
Peterson, D., *Thomas Jefferson*. New York: Hill and Wang, 1967.
Rosenberger, Francis Coleman, *Jefferson Reader*. New York: E. P. Dutton & Company, 1953.

AMERICAN HISTORY

Brooks, Van Wyck, *The World of Washington Irving*. New York: E. P. Dutton & Company, 1944.
Encyclopaedia Britannica, The Annals of America, Vol. II, 1968.
Miller, John C., *Origins of the American Revolution*. Boston: Little, Brown & Company, 1943.
Morrison, Samuel Eliot, *The Oxford History of the American People*. New York: Oxford University Press, 1965.
Mowat, Charles Loch, *East Florida as a British Province, 1763–1784*. Gainesville: University of Florida Press, 1964.
Rossiter, Clinton, *The Grand Convention*. New York: The Macmillan Company, 1966.
Russell, Francis, *The French and Indian Wars*. New York: Harper & Row, 1965.

NORTH CAROLINA HISTORY

Cooper, Arthur W. and Satterthwaite, Sheafe, *Smith Island and the Cape Fear Peninsula*. Raleigh: Wildlife Preserves, 1964.
Frome, Michael, *Strangers in High Places*. New York: Doubleday & Company, 1966.
Lee, Lawrence, *The Lower Cape Fear in Colonial Days*. Chapel Hill: University of North Carolina Press, 1965.
Lefler, Hugh Talmage and Newsome, Albert Ray, *North Carolina: The History of a Southern State*. Chapel Hill: University of North Carolina Press, 1963.
Ross, Malcolm, *The Cape Fear*. New York: Holt, Rinehart and Winston, 1965.

OTHER HISTORY

Cabell, James Branch and Hanna, Alfred Jackson, *The St. Johns.* New York: Farrar & Rinehart, 1943.

Churchill, Winston S., *A History of the English Speaking Peoples,* Vol. III. New York: Dodd, Mead & Company, 1964.

Durant, Will and Ariel, *The Age of Voltaire.* New York: Simon & Schuster, 1965.

The Journals of Lewis & Clark. New York: The Heritage Press, 1962.

NATURAL HISTORY

Brockman, C. Frank, *Trees of North America.* New York: Golden Press, 1968.

Farb, Peter, *Face of North America.* New York: Harper & Row, 1963.

Harrar, Ellwood S. and J. George, *Guide to Southern Trees.* New York: Dover Publications, 1962.

Palmer, E. Laurence, *Fieldbook of Natural History.* New York: McGraw-Hill Book Company, 1949.

Romans, Bernard, *Natural History of Florida* (1775). Gainesville: University of Florida Press, 1962.

Shelford, Victor E., *The Ecology of North America.* Urbana: University of Illinois Press, 1963.

Wells, B. W., *The Natural Gardens of North Carolina.* Chapel Hill: University of North Carolina Press, 1967.

BIRDS

Audubon, John James, *The Birds of America.* New York: The Macmillan Company, 1937.

The Original Water-color Paintings of John James Audubon. New York: American Heritage Publishing Company, 1966.

Bailey, Harold H., *The Birds of Florida.* Baltimore: Williams & Wilkins, 1925.

Burleigh, Thomas D., *Georgia Birds.* Norman: University of Oklahoma Press, 1958.

Chamberlain, Montague, *Nuttall's Ornithology.* Boston: Little, Brown & Company, 1891.

Forbush, Edward Howe, *Natural History of the Birds of Eastern and Central North America*. Boston: Houghton Mifflin Company, 1939.

Sprunt, Alexander, Jr., *Florida Bird Life*. New York: Coward-McCann, 1954.

——, *South Carolina Bird Life*. Columbia: University of South Carolina Press, 1949.

Wilson, Alexander, *American Ornithology*. Philadelphia, 1808–1814.

GARDENS

Clark, H. F., *The English Landscape Garden*. London: Pleiades Books Ltd., 1948.

Coats, Peter, *Great Gardens of the Western World*. New York: G. P. Putnam's Sons, 1963.

Fairbrother, Nan, *Men and Gardens*. New York: Alfred A. Knopf, 1956.

Fisher, Louise B., *An Eighteenth Century Garland*. Williamsburg: Colonial Williamsburg, 1951.

Hadfield, Miles, *Pioneers in Gardening*. New York: The Macmillan Company.

Hyams, Edward, *The English Garden*. New York: Harry N. Abrams, 1966.

Robinson, W., *The English Flower Garden*. London: John Murray, 1907.

Wright, Richardson, *The Story of Gardening*. New York: Dover Publications, 1963.

CRITICISM

Coleridge, Samuel Taylor, *Biographia Literaria*. New York: E. P. Dutton & Company, 1952.

Huxley, Aldous, *Literature and Science*. New York: Harper & Row, 1963.

Lowes, John Livingston, *The Road to Xanadu*. Boston: Houghton Mifflin Company, 1927.

Peattie, Donald Culross, *An Almanac for Moderns*. New York: G. P. Putnam's Sons, 1935.

Philadelphia Botanical Club, *Bartonia*. Philadelphia: Academy of Natural Sciences, 1931.

Swem, E. G., "Brothers of the Spade," *Barre* (Massachusetts) *Gazette*. American Antiquarian Society, 1957.

Thornton, James, *Table Talk: From Ben Jonson to Leigh Hunt*. London: J. M. Dent & Sons Ltd., 1934.

Williams, William Carlos, *In the American Grain*. New York: New Directions, 1956.

Index

WILLIAM BARTRAM (1739–1823) was the son of John Bartram, Royal Botanist to King George III, and friend of Benjamin Franklin, George Washington, and Thomas Jefferson. Growing up in the famous Philadelphia garden of his father, William developed an early interest in the plants, birds, turtles, and other wildlife that he found there on the banks of the Schuylkill.

As a boy, he neglected his schoolwork and later his storekeeping to follow birds through the woods and draw them, and to help his father collect the roots and seeds that were sent across the ocean on sailing ships for the gardens of the nobility of England.

Because he could not seem to settle down and learn a trade, he was sometimes called "Poor Billy." Yet his father and Mr. Franklin understood his longing to wander through the wilderness, and they found for him a British patron who sponsored an expedition into the southeast and as far west as the Mississippi.

While on this journey, Billy Bartram continued to sketch the wildlife he found on every side, and to keep the journal that, safely back home in his father's garden, he later expanded into his classic book, *The Travels*.

As America's first native-born ornithologist, he compiled a list of 215 birds, and influenced the art of Alexander Wilson and John James Audubon. As America's first ecologist, he understood the value of observing a plant or animal in its own environment rather than simply as an isolated specimen. Thomas Jeffer-